Merry Christmas Ben!
2013

RATMAN

The Trial and Conviction of Whitey Bulger

HOWIE CARR

Frandel, LLC

Howie Carr

Table of Contents

Acknowledgments

So many people contributed to the production of this book in such a short amount of time that I hope I don't miss thanking anyone who should be included in this brief list.

First of all, my wife Kathy, who handled all the production details—the partnership with Bookmasters, cover design, new magnets, the book-signing schedule, etc. If you're getting—or giving—this book as a Christmas present, think of Kathy. Without her prodding and pushing, this book might have made a perfect gift—for Father's Day.

My three daughters—Carolyn, Charlotte and Tina—all helped their computer-challenged father in varying amounts, with varying amounts of snide remarks about my Stone Age ways.

Outside of the family, I certainly owe most to my radio producer, Nancy "Sandy" Shack, who kept track of an immense amount of exhibits, mainly photographs, that arrived daily from the courthouse. She also deciphered my scribbling and made sure every picture ended up where it belonged in the text. I can't thank you enough, Sandy.

Mark Garfinkel, the *Boston Herald's* great photographer, is responsible for most of the photographs in *Ratman* that were taken outside the courthouse. I thank Mark and his fellow *Herald* photographers, who sometimes took such riveting photos that my column in the newspaper the next morning was superfluous. (I'm thinking Kevin O'Neil.) Also at the *Herald*, thanks to head photographers Jim Mahoney and Arthur Pollock, who tracked down my ancient mug shots, and head librarian Martha Reagan, who almost always found the obscure, 50-year-old clipping that I'd requested.

Thanks too to the *Herald*'s publisher Pat Purcell, editor Joe Sciacca and managing editor John Strahinich for running such a great paper that I could spend most of the summer on basically one subject, day after day after day. And when I couldn't make it to court, *Herald* reporter Laurel J. Sweet always kept me up-to-date with her notes.

Another *Herald* stalwart, Tyrell Adamson, produced a great cover, working with the three traditional true-crime colors, red, white and black.

Sincere gratitude goes to Anthony Amore of the Isabella Stewart Gardner Museum, who read behind me and served as a kind of line editor. I appreciate Christina Sterling from the U.S. Attorney's office for her prompt daily delivery of all the latest exhibits, and for a phone call one Friday night in June that I will always remember—telling me that as one of Whitey's defense witnesses I was now "sequestered," i.e., banned from the courtroom. (Thank you, Judge Casper, for letting me back in on Monday morning.) Thanks also to professional proofreader and technical editor Wes Wilson for editing the galleys one final time before *Ratman* went to press.

Thanks too to all my radio affiliates that supported my *Night of Crime* tour, which served as a launching pad for both *Rifleman* and *Ratman*. Cary Pahigian, Jeff Wade, and Warren Maddock at WGAN, Sean Davey at WHYN, Sheila and Bob Vinikoor at WNTK, Bruce Biette at WVOM, Kurt Carberry at WCRN, Bob Cox at WKBK and Allison Makkay Davis at WXTK—I trust we'll all continue to be together, well into the future.

At Bookmasters, I couldn't ask for a better project director than Jen Welsch. Her turnaround time is astonishing. Thanks also to Ray Sevin, who keeps the schedule running smoothly, Tony Proe and Jon Ackerman in sales, and our customer services rep, Elaine Lattanzi. Mike Dever is a master of production; his skill is the reason you're holding this book in your hands so soon after the trial.

As always, many others helped out, but it would be doing them a disservice to name them. Those are my "sources."

So this is it, the end of a long run, sometimes scary, more often fun (especially after Ratman went on the lam). If you want to know more about the other books (they're all still in print) go to my website howiecarrshow.com. I hope you enjoy this fourth and final volume of the series, and I'll end with the two words that I originally wanted to use as the title of this book:

Goodbye, Whitey.

Howie Carr

Prologue

Whitey with James Stephen Martorano

THIS IS JAMES J. "Whitey" Bulger, Jr. in 1986, at the height of his underworld career, a literal "godfather" for the youngest son of his underworld partner John Martorano. This photo was taken at St. Clement's Church in Somerville, or, as Martorano nonchalantly described it at Whitey's trial, "somewhere in Boston."

Johnny—"the Cook," as Whitey called him—had named his infant son James Stephen: James after Whitey and Stephen after Stevie "the Rifleman" Flemmi. They were the three remaining partners in the Winter Hill Gang, of which Whitey had become the dominant member.

"Overbearing," Flemmi would describe Whitey in court in 2013.

His job in the gang? "Intimidation, mostly," Martorano would say in court in 2008.

But in 1986, Whitey was on top o' the world, Ma, top o' the world, as his cinematic hero Jimmy Cagney put it in *White Heat*. His younger brother Billy was the most powerful politician in the state; when a colonel in the State Police put a bug in Whitey's garage, an anonymous rider was quickly added to the state budget to force his retirement. Another state cop who stopped Whitey from taking cash out of the country at Logan Airport was summarily transferred to the sticks after the cop refused to hand over his police report to the head of the airport, an appointee of the 1988 Democratic nominee for president, Gov. Michael S. Dukakis.

Whitey was the biggest cocaine dealer in his hometown of South Boston, if not the entire city, yet the *Boston Globe*'s columnists insisted that he had "kept the drugs out of Southie."

He had six FBI agents on his payroll, not to mention untold local cops. He was making so many payoffs to the police that he coined a saying that would become famous in Boston in the years ahead:

"Christmas is for cops and kids."

The cops came in handy. Gangsters have always shaken down other criminals, but in Whitey Bulger's Boston, even law-abiding citizens had nowhere to turn when they found Whitey pointing a gun at them. One businessman, Michael Solimando, a partner of one of the gang's murder victims, was summoned to Whitey's bar in the Lower End in 1982. Whitey demanded $400,000 that he falsely claimed he was owed by the murdered businessman. Whitey pointed a gun at Solimando's head, then put the gun down and grabbed a machine gun and shoved it into his victim's crotch.

As Solimando recalled in August 2013:

"He said, you know, 'If you think you could—if you're going to law enforcement,' he said, 'we're going to know the minute you walk on the 14th floor of the Federal building. We're going to know about it. And if you think you're going to go to the State Police, forget about it. We're covered there. And forget about the Boston P.D. We're going to know. We're going to know the minute you open your mouth. And what we're going to do is get a hat, put three names it, all right? And we're going to pull one name, all right, and that guy's going to be dead. And then we'll see how fast the other two come up with the money.'"

How about the Witness Protection Program? Whitey had anticipated that question too. "We'd find you," he told Solimando.

Then Whitey told Solimando personal details about his two partners, one of whom was married to Solimando's sister. She owned horses in Milton.

"Tell your sister to sell the hay burners," Whitey said, using an archaic term for horses. "Get the money."

He and his partners got the money all right—$400,000. And when Solimando was called before a grand jury, like so many others he felt he had to commit perjury if he wanted to survive. He denied Whitey had extorted the money from him. When he was called back to testify a second time, the gang gave Solimando police mug shots of another extortion victim, whom they'd murdered and buried in a basement. They told Solimando to blame the shakedown on the "missing" guy.

"You'll never have to worry about it," Solimando was told. "He'll never come back at you."

Whitey had obtained the mug shots from one of "his" FBI agents, a guy named Zip Connolly. Zip supplied Whitey with the latest information on everything the law was doing; and he was soon on the gang's payroll.

"I'm in the gang!" he bragged after one $25,000 payoff, and he began spending his bribe money so recklessly that Whitey and Stevie eventually had to cut him off.

"We'd still pay him," Stevie explained, "but he had to tell us what he needed it for."

In other words, they weren't just bribing the police. They had them on allowances, as if they were children.

In this blurred defense photo, Whitey relaxes with defrocked pederast priest, Monsignor Fred Ryan

A couple of years before Whitey posed for his "godfather" photo, a new mayor had been elected in Boston, Ray Flynn. Like the Bulgers, he was from Southie. Billy Bulger knew how much a Boston mayor needed friends in the legislature—for financial aid, new taxes, the right appointments to the state-controlled watchdog agencies, etc. Senate president Bulger called Ray Flynn and said he'd do whatever he could for his Southie neighbor, and that he only asked one favor in return.

He wanted Zip Connolly appointed police commissioner.

Flynn blanched. He knew who—and what—Zip Connolly was. Anything else he would do, Mayor-elect Flynn told the Senate president. But Police Commissioner Connolly? No way. So for years Billy blocked anything Flynn wanted done on Beacon Hill, in addition to missing no opportunity to demean him personally in public. Instead Flynn appointed a guy named Francis "Mickey" Roache. By a coincidence, Roache's brother was a gangster who had been paralyzed when he was shot by Whitey in a West Broadway ginmill owned by a bookie named Bobby Ford, who would later sell his home in Thomas Park in Southie to Zip Connolly. . . .

Those were the days, my friend, they thought they'd never end. But not really. As early as 1977, Whitey began setting up false identities for himself, just in case he eventually had to go on the lam. He wasn't going back to jail, that much he knew. He'd done nine years in federal prisons for bank robbery between 1956 and 1965, and would have done a lot more time if

Young Whitey and his first gang, circa 1940

he hadn't ratted out two other members of his gang. Which was another one of his dirty little secrets—that he was an informer, a rat, and had been since 1956. His brother wrote a cloying memoir in 1996 in which he dwelt on how their predominantly Irish hometown of Southie "loathed informers." Every year, at one of his little Irish men's club dinners, Billy Bulger would present an award to an absent person, usually a politician, whom he considered to have betrayed him in the past year.

It was called the Gypo Nolan Award, after the title character of the Liam O'Flaherty novel *The Informer* that John Ford made into an Oscar-winning 1935 movie. Gypo was the informer, the rat, who turned in his best pal to the Black and Tans for a 20-pound bounty.

By 1986, the Gypo Nolan bullshit from the Bulgers was wearing thin, even at the *Globe*. Whitey had belonged to the Winter Hill Gang, which had been decimated by a race-fixing scandal in which he and his fellow FBI informer Stevie Flemmi had been named as "unindicted coconspirators." Then the Mafia—"In Town," as it was known—had been decapitated by FBI bugs on which the names of Whitey and Stevie were mentioned repeatedly. But their corrupt FBI agents had made sure to list them on the Title III warrants as informants. And that immunized them from prosecution on any evidence produced by the bugs placed in Mafia boss Jerry Angiulo's headquarters. And now a new generation of Mafioso were about to be taken down on yet another FBI bug, this one in a bakery at the Prudential Center.

As their rivals and even ostensible allies like Johnny Martorano were imprisoned or went on the lam, Whitey and Stevie skated, growing ever richer with their extortions, their drugs, and the "rent" they shook down from both bookies and large-scale drug dealers.

But cracks were beginning to appear. Embarrassed by its obsequious coverage over the years, the *Globe* assigned a team of reporters to investigate Whitey's "special relationship" with the FBI. Zip Connolly's boss, who had accepted $7,000 from Whitey, blurted out to a reporter, "You have no idea how dangerous he is!" Another allegedly "comprised" FBI agent warned a second *Globe* reporter that Whitey would not hesitate to kill him if the planned series of articles ran. The bent fed cited as his source a Winter Hill associate conveniently unavailable for confirmation, due to his disappearance into the Witness Protection Program.

The *Globe* series finally ran, in September 1988. It was called "The Bulger Mystique," and it covered both Whitey and Billy. Billy Bulger said his brother was always welcome at his home, and that "there is much to admire" about him.

"He's supposed to be just the toughest guy," Billy said with pride. "A very, very determined, formidable person."

Formidable—the same word Stevie Flemmi would use under oath 25 years later. Along with "overbearing."

The paper didn't actually out him as an informant, but the words "special relationship" left little doubt. Fugitive Johnny Martorano called Stevie from Florida asking what was going on, and Flemmi gave him the party line—that the *Globe* was out to get Billy, not Whitey.

But by now, the feds—minus the FBI, of course—had opened a new line of investigation. They began going after the bookmakers who had been paying "rent" to Whitey, and especially Stevie, for years. At first they dummied up, then they were granted immunity, and when the bookies still wouldn't talk, they were handed 18-month prison sentences for contempt. The feds began talking about "forfeitures."

"What is this, Russia?" one aging bookie complained to his lawyer in court. Finally they were more scared of somebody than Stevie Flemmi. Soon Boston bookies began vanishing into the Witness Protection program.

In 1990, the feds opened another front in their expanding war against what was now known as the Bulger Group. Another non-FBI investigation took down Whitey's cocaine operation. Fifty dealers, but not Whitey, were arrested, many of them at their public sector jobs. One was collared while sleeping overnight on his "job" at the city's Department of Public Works yard on Frontage Road. In the morning he had been scheduled to report to his second public-sector job, at a state agency where the hiring was controlled by the wife of one of Billy Bulger's most loyal senators, who had once assaulted a political opponent for passing out leaflets linking him to the Bulgers.

That afternoon, the Drug Enforcement Administration (DEA) held a press conference.

"For years the Bulger organization has told people there's no drugs in Southie," said a DEA agent, "that Southie boys are not involved in drugs, that we throw drug dealers out of here. These arrests show that that's not true. These arrests show the people have been had by James 'Whitey' Bulger."

It would only take the feds 21 more years to arrest him.

IN THE fall 1990 elections, nine of Billy Bulger's Democrat senators were ousted in the Republican landslide that brought in a GOP governor whose ads had featured Billy Bulger's face morphing into Whitey's. Zip Connolly, their go-to guy in the FBI, abruptly retired to take a six-figure job with a state utility that needed to keep friendly relations with state government—that is, Billy Bulger. Whitey and Stevie gave Zip a final retirement gift—$10,000 cash.

Still, the situation seemed manageable—in the summer of 1991, the brother of one of Whitey's gunsels won the $14.3-million Mass Millions lottery. Whitey and two of his hoodlums claimed shares, and had to show up at Lottery headquarters in Braintree. They were videotaped by the surveillance cameras, Whitey wearing a white Red Sox cap and sunglasses. The photo ran on the national wires; suddenly everyone in Massachusetts, and the nation, knew what the mysterious Whitey looked like. His photo, with an arrow helpfully pointing him out, appeared on the front page of *USA Today*. *GQ* ran a feature article about him. But what could Whitey do? There were too many reporters covering him now to threaten them all.

In the old days, the Winter Hill Gang had been known for taking care of its members who went to jail. Even Mafia members sometimes got more assistance from Howie Winter and Johnny Martorano than from In Town. But now, multimillionaire Whitey turned his back on his imprisoned drug dealers. They began flipping too.

The indictments came down in December 1994. Zip got the tip from another of their FBI pals and passed it along to Whitey, who immediately fled. Stevie Flemmi dallied, and a week later was arrested by DEA agents coming out of his son's restaurant. He was stunned.

"What is this, a grandstand play?" he complained. Asked if he wanted to call a lawyer, he instead phoned an FBI agent. He asked his G-man friend to get him out; the fed offered him a Coke instead. The golden era was over.

But Whitey was gone. He returned to Boston briefly a few weeks later to drop off his older girlfriend and exchange her for a younger one, Catherine Greig, a dental hygienist 22 years his junior. Then they began traveling, aimlessly. For 18 months, the FBI couldn't be bothered to interview the first girlfriend, but when they finally did in mid-1996, she gave up Whitey's alias, Tom Baxter. It turned out "Tom Baxter" had been stopped by cops twice in 1995–96—in Mississippi and in Wyoming. But now he needed new IDs. He called his last remaining underling, Kevin Weeks, and eventually obtained some usable fake IDs. Weeks saw his "mentor" for the last time in 1996 at "the Lions," their description of the New York Public Library.

"Anything happens," Whitey said, "put it on me."

Little did he know . . . A year later, trying to have the indictments thrown out, Stevie Flemmi admitted he had been an FBI informant since the 1960's. Whitey was outed as well. Meanwhile Flemmi, still imprisoned at the Plymouth County Correctional Facility, vainly tried to explain to his fellow defendants why he and Whitey had become rats.

"You don't understand," he told them. "They gave us gold, and we gave them shit."

The others immediately understood: they had been the shit. Johnny Martorano soon disappeared from the pod where they all were held; he was cutting a deal to testify against Whitey and Stevie and Zip. Martorano began listing murder after murder after murder—and he hadn't even been in Boston for the mob's final spree.

Zip Connolly was indicted in 1999, as was Kevin Weeks, who flipped a mere two weeks after his arrest, thereby earning himself the nickname "Two Weeks." Weeks knew where the bodies were buried. Soon six victims, including two of Stevie's girlfriends, were recovered from shallow graves on public land. Weeks also revealed that Billy Bulger, now the president of the University of Massachusetts, had been in contact with his brother after he fled. Billy was summoned to a grand jury but avoided the perjury trap, admitting that he had been called by Whitey at the home of one of his Senate employees in Quincy.

Another Boston FBI scandal was simultaneously unfolding. In 1968, the FBI had remained silent as four Mafia members and associates were convicted of a murder the FBI knew they had not committed. The Bureau had looked the other way to protect the first mobster they'd recruited into the Witness Protection Program—Joe Barboza, a Portuguese hitman for In Town who had turned against his Mafia masters.

The four innocent men all served at least 30 years. Two, including a World War II hero, died in prison.

It was a national story, covered by *60 Minutes*. When Congressional hearings were held, the focus quickly spread to the question of Whitey and Billy Bulger, even though Whitey had still been a few days from being released from prison when the murder occurred and the FBI cover-up began. In December 2002, Billy Bulger was subpoenaed to appear before the House Committee on Government Reform in Boston. He leaked word that he might defy the subpoena and not appear. That infuriated the new Republican governor-elect, Mitt Romney, who ordered Bulger to attend.

Billy began by reading from a 19th-century court decision about the "ambiguous circumstances" decent men sometimes find themselves in. Then the committee chairman asked him the first question, "Do you know where your brother is?"

Billy Bulger took the Fifth Amendment.

In June of 2003, Billy appeared before the committee again, this time in Washington and with a grant of immunity. Still, he desperately tried to avoid answering the congressmen's questions, often resorting to such convoluted replies as, "To the best of my recollection I cannot recall."

Asked about his 1996 memoirs, in which he fulsomely praised Whitey and said that most of the allegations against him were either "purchased" or "tabloid talk-show stuff in Boston," Billy backed off his staunch defense.

"At the time," he said, "there was no talk of the more terrible crimes."

The hearing, televised live on all the major TV stations back in Boston, effectively ended William M. Bulger's career. But like his older brother, Billy too had planned ahead: once it appeared that he might lose his job, his loyal lackeys on the university board of trustees had given him a three-year contract extension. Billy walked away in the fall of 1996 with a $900,000 severance check and a $200,000-a-year state pension. He immediately filed with the State Retirement Board demanding a $29,000 increase in his state pension, his "kiss in the mail," as it was called in South Boston.

Meanwhile, the trail left behind by Whitey grew ever colder, despite at least one feature a year on the television series *America's Most Wanted,* as well as an annual FBI press conference in Boston on his birthday, Sept. 3. In 1996 he was placed on the FBI's Most Wanted List, and eventually a reward of $1 million, later increased to $2 million, was put on his head. In London, police discovered a Barclays Bank branch where years earlier Whitey had stashed $50,000 cash in a safe-deposit box, as well as the key to yet another safe-deposit box in Dublin. When the branch was relocated in 1997, a call had been placed to the contact number Whitey had left behind. It rang in Billy Bulger's house in South Boston.

"James Bulger's current whereabouts are unknown," said an unidentified woman before hanging up.

After the 9/11 terror attacks of 2001, it became conventional wisdom that the new, more stringent security measures had trapped the two fugitives somewhere in the European Union. In June 2004, on the 60th anniversary of D-Day, FBI agents scanned the crowds at Normandy, thinking World War II buff Whitey (he was a Nazi fan) might put in an appearance. He did not.

Meanwhile, occasional sightings of the phantom fugitive were still reported in the U.S. In Boston, the FBI set up a Violent Fugitive Task Force to handle the tips, but over the years the squad dwindled in size. The law-enforcement infighting that had always proven so fortuitous to Whitey continued. In 2000, the FBI office in LA sent out a fax to the press announcing a confirmed sighting of Whitey at a beauty parlor in southern California, where he was supposedly spotted picking up Catherine after a hair appointment. Two hours later, the Boston FBI office issued its own fax, claiming there had been no such sighting.

By 2011, Whitey seemed to be fading into American criminal lore. Of course, the only way to become a true legend is vanish permanently, never to reappear, like a handful of earlier Americans, both criminal and otherwise— Judge Crater, Amelia Earhart, Ambrose Bierce, Jimmy Hoffa and D.B. Cooper, among others. Whitey, it appeared, would go down in history, to be recalled in an endless series of books claiming to "solve" the mystery, each one selling fewer copies as those who remembered him firsthand died off.

For Whitey, it really was

But then the U.S. Marshals were invited to take a run at Whitey. In recent years, they had built a reputation—and solidified their niche in federal law-enforcement—for tracking down cold-case fugitives. They took a new look at the Bulger case and concluded that, contrary to earlier theories, Whitey and Catherine had probably never fled the country after they flew from Chicago to New York in 1996 and the trail went cold.

In May 2011, Osama bin Laden was finally taken down in Pakistan by SEAL Team Six. In Santa Monica, CA, an octogenarian named "Charles Gasko" watched the news on cable TV and then turned to his wife "Carol," and said, "This is it."

Now Charles Gasko—also known as Whitey Bulger—would be number one on the FBI's Most Wanted List.

Since at least 1995, Charles and Carol Gasko had been leasing the $1,165-a-month rent-controlled Unit 303 in the Princess Eugenia apartment building a few blocks from the beach. In 2007, a visiting Las Vegas man who had watched the most recent *America's Most Wanted* segment reported seeing him on the Santa Monica boardwalk. The sighting was still listed on the television program's log book.

In mid-June 2011, amid much media skepticism, the marshals announced a new campaign to catch Whitey. It was a relatively low-budget affair, buying daytime-TV spots on shows likely to be watched by females in the same age group as Catherine Greig, who had just turned 60. The ads featured Greig, and prominently mentioned the $2 million reward. The marshals bought runs in San Diego and San Francisco, but opted to pass on the prohibitively expensive LA market.

But CNN International decided to run a feature on the new campaign, and in Iceland, a late-middle-aged model named Anna Bjornsdottir watched as she saw two people she immediately recognized. A former Miss Iceland, Bjornsdottir had been featured in the famous "Take-It-Off" Noxzema shaving-cream ads of the 1970's. She still worked as a model in Hollywood several months a year, and maintained an apartment at the Princess Eugenia.

Like Carol Gasko, she loved animals, and one morning several years earlier had noticed Carol Gasko feeding a stray cat named Tiger at dawn. Tiger had belonged to a neighbor who died, and none of the other residents could coax the feline inside. The only person the cat seemed to trust was Carol, who took to feeding Tiger milk twice a day. Bjornsdottir stopped to chat, and the two became casual friends; eventually she was introduced to Mr. Gasko, an odd, standoffish duck, 20-plus years older than Carol.

Still, they all got along until one morning in early 2009, when Bjornsdottir mentioned how fortunate America was to have a new young, black president. Whitey instantly flew into a rage, screaming about the "nigger" in the White House and how the races should never mix. Carol listened in silence as her "husband" continued his racist fulminations.

A few days later, thinking he must have calmed down, Bjornsdottir approached Charlie again, but he refused to speak to her. In fact, he never spoke to her again.

In Iceland, as soon as the CNN segment was over, Bjornsdottir reached for her phone and dialed the number she'd seen on the TV screen. She was quickly connected with Boston, and the agents suspected they'd hit pay dirt when they ran a nationwide identity check and discovered no one named either Charles or Carol Gasko.

In Los Angeles, the FBI agent assigned to fugitives, Scott Garriola, worked mainly with the LAPD. He had a gruff, Joe Friday just-the-facts big-city cop style—a bracing contrast to the slightly shady parade of Boston FBI agents who would take the witness stand in the summer of 2013. Garriola was on vacation, but as soon as he got the call he excitedly called a babysitter and drove out to Santa Monica with four Los Angeles cops. It didn't take them long to realize they had their man, or actually their woman, because since bin Laden's takedown, Whitey had become a virtual recluse. On the door of their apartment was a hand-lettered sign: DO NOT KNOCK UNDER ANY CIRCUMSTANCES.

Garriola went to the apartment manager, a 27-year-old Mississippi native named Josh Bond who lived next door to the Gaskos. Even though he'd gone to Boston University, he had no inkling that Charlie Gasko was anybody other than, well, some garrulous old man who seemed a little too interested in him, showering him with gifts—half-bottles of cognac, Stetson cowboy hats, free weights, a coffee table book of Elvis Presley photographs and, most recently, a beard-trimmer.

Bond later told the FBI: "If BOND had not thought the GASKO's (sic) were such a nice old couple, he would have thought that CHARLIE was trying to get BOND in shape because he (CHARLIE) was attracted to him."

When he arrived at Bond's little office, Garriola showed him photographs of the two fugitives.

"He buried his head in his hands and he started shaking his head," Garriola testified at Whitey's trial. "He immediately said, 'These are my neighbors.'"

He told Garriola he was "100 percent certain" that the Gaskos were in fact the Bulgers. As a BU grad, he'd recognized their Boston accents, even though Mr. Gasko claimed they were from Chicago and New York.

Garriola and Bond discussed possible ways to get them out of the apartment—turning off the power, knocking on the door, telling them there was a gas leak, etc. Bond didn't think they'd fall for any of those corny old gags. They were in the garage brainstorming when Garriola noticed a group of lockers that tenants used to store their possessions. Garriola suggested that Bond call Unit 303, tell them their locker had been broken into, and that they needed to come down and see if anything was missing before he called the police. Whitey wouldn't want the police coming around.

Bond agreed that might work, so Garriola went out to his car, got his bolt cutters and chopped the lock off Whitey's locker. Then he told Bond to go make the call. There was no answer in the apartment, but about five minutes later Carol called Bond back and said Whitey—er, Charles—was coming right down to the basement. Garriola and his LAPD cops were ready.

As soon as the elevator door opened, Garriola and three cops approached Whitey. They told him to get his hands up.

"We asked him to get down on his knees on the ground and—I mean, he swore at us a few times, told us he wasn't going to get down on his knees, there was grease on the floor, things like that. There was an exchange back and forth, harsh words back and forth."

As Whitey later described it in a letter from the jail: "More threats. Loud. Guns shaking a bit."

Finally he dropped to his knees. The cops handcuffed him and Garriola asked him his name.

Whitey replied, Charles Gasko. Then he asked Garriola to identify himself, which he did, after which Garriola asked him, "Are you Whitey Bulger?"

"At first he wouldn't admit it. I told him then we'd have to go upstairs and see if there was any ID in your apartment, maybe Catherine can identify you. He says, 'You know who I am.' He says, 'I'm Whitey Bulger.'"

Then they went upstairs and got Catherine, and brought her down to the garage. Garriola wanted to search the apartment, and he didn't want to have to wait for a search warrant. So he asked Whitey if he'd sign a consent form—an FBI FD 26. Whitey agreed; he told Garriola that he would be as cooperative as necessary, and that he hoped that this would count toward some sort of future consideration for Catherine. Garriola told Whitey he'd tell his superiors about his cooperation, and the reasons why.

Garriola handed Whitey the search-consent form to sign, and he did, then gave the form back to the FBI agent.

"He said, 'It's the first time I've signed this name in a long time.' "
The prosecutor asked, "And the name he signed the form with was?"
"James J. Bulger."
It was June 22, 2011.

Whitey arrives at court via helicopter in hand and ankle cuffs,
June 2011

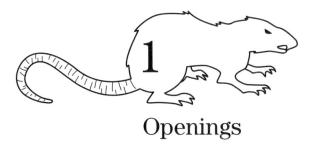

Openings

It was June 12, 2013.

"Thank you, your Honor," said Brian Kelly, the assistant U.S. attorney who would deliver the prosecution's opening statement in the case of *United States of America v. James J. Bulger, Jr.* "Good morning."

Finally, in Courtroom 11 on the fifth floor of the J. Joseph Moakley Courthouse, Whitey Bulger's racketeering and murder trial was about to begin.

Much had happened in the almost two years since Whitey's arrest in Santa Monica. His girlfriend, Catherine Greig, had pleaded guilty in 2012 to harboring a fugitive and was serving an eight-year sentence in a federal penitentiary in Waseca, MN. Her scheduled release date is June 10, 2018. She was also ordered to forfeit $150,000, which forced her to sell the home Whitey had bought for her so many years ago in Quincy.

A Santa Monica neighbor reported that Whitey had written him from jail that he'd somehow heard from his moll when she was being held in Central Falls, RI before her guilty plea.

"She told him she doesn't regret the 16 years she lived with him. And he doesn't either."

Greig wanted poster

Inside the love nest in Santa Monica, cops discovered an incredible cache of weapons, ranging from machine guns and double-shot derringers to illegal double-edged "push knives"—essentially brass knuckles with a knife that fit into the palm, perfect for driving into a victim's sternum, or heart. The "Gaskos" had also become hoarders—they had enough dry goods stashed to last at least a decade. They even stockpiled multiple pairs of identical shoes.

Inside an old-fashioned Boston wall "hide," the FBI also discovered $822,000 in cash, in mostly new bills. On the day they had their first hearings in federal court in Boston, a lien was placed on that $822,000 by a lawyer for the former owner of the South Boston Liquor Mart, which Whitey had extorted from her. She had already won a legal judgment against Whitey for millions in lost income.

Thus, Whitey could claim to be indigent, and he did. The taxpayers would be paying for his defense.

Both of Whitey's brothers, Billy and Jackie, appeared at their older brother's first court appearance in Boston. After the arrest, the former state Senate and UMass president had issued a statement to the press: "I wish to express my sympathy to all the families hurt by the calamitous circumstances of this case."

Guns recovered at Whitey's Santa Monica apartment

Jackie and Billy Bulger at federal courthouse, 2011

But the reporters wanted something on videotape, and after the hearing, out on Northern Avenue, Billy was chased by TV camera crews until he was finally surrounded. Shoving a microphone into his face, a TV reporter noted that in the courtroom Billy had seemed "emotional." Billy thought for a moment, then nodded in agreement.

"These are," he said, "unusual circumstances."

As Whitey's lawyer, the court appointed J.W. Carney, whose earlier clients had included Brookline abortion-clinic shooter John Salvi, a convicted would-be Muslim mall-bomber terrorist, and a radio-station employee who had poisoned his wife with anti-freeze. At every opportunity, Carney assured reporters that his client would definitely be testifying in his own defense.

The Bulger case would turn out to be an extremely lucrative assignment for Carney. After the trial, his billing records were released, and through June, Carney and his firm had already received $2.7 million for their representation. And that didn't even include the future bills that would still be tendered, for the rest of the actual trial, followed by the sentencing, the appeals . . .

Whitey was jailed at Plymouth County Correctional Facility, the same place where his partners-in-crime had been incarcerated 16 years earlier. Now, except for Flemmi, they were all free men once more, and only one, Robert DeLuca, was in the Witness Protection Program.

Whitey was held in solitary confinement, and at first correctional officers competed to stand guard outside his cell 24 hours a day. But the duty soon seemed a chore; instead of one of America's legendary gangsters, the guards found themselves sitting across from an old man who never stopped yapping. Some used the same verb to describe his incessant inane chattering that Josh Bond had used when he was interviewed by the FBI—"droning."

He told the bored guards that Plymouth was worse than Alcatraz. He bitched about the food, the fat guards, and the twice-daily strip searches. He described Johnny Martorano as a "bully"—much to Martorano's amusement.

In December 2011 Whitey complained of chest pains and was transported by ambulance to Boston Medical Center, which is known for its trauma center. As he was wheeled into the emergency room, Whitey was given an alias to confuse any would-be assassins—Perry Mason. But "Perry Mason" refused to take off his shirt for an EKG and was immediately driven back to Plymouth.

Meanwhile, Whitey's attorney Carney immediately began seeking continuance after continuance, accusing the feds of holding back some of the voluminous discovery in the case. He also asked the first judge assigned to the case to recuse himself because of his work as an assistant U.S. attorney in the 1980's. Eventually the judge was replaced—by a black woman named Denise J. Casper. It seemed an ironic switch, given Whitey's disdain for blacks, especially the one who had appointed her to the federal bench, Barack H. Obama.

Carney announced that he would be filing a motion detailing how a certain unnamed fed had given Whitey immunity from prosecution for any crimes, up to and including murder. When Carney finally filed the motion, it turned out that Whitey claimed he had been granted this 007 license by the former head of the Organized Crime Strike Force, Jeremiah O'Sullivan. O'Sullivan was conveniently deceased, but before his death had denied giving Whitey Bulger any sort of immunity.

In another attempt to delay his client's trial, Carney told the court that preparation was taking much longer than originally anticipated, not just because of the 300,000 pages of discovery, but because Whitey now refused

Federal prosecutors Jeremiah O'Sullivan and Diane Kottmyer,
future state judge

to discuss the case on the phone, believing that his phone was tapped and his correspondence routinely opened.

"James Bulger has a view," Carney wrote, "based on his personal experience, that all levels of law enforcement are corrupt and will disregard the law if it suits them."

But finally the trial could be delayed no longer. Carney's witness list included 82 names, among them five reporters Whitey viewed as unfriendly, including the author of this book. As potential witnesses, the reporters would be "sequestered," i.e., kept out of the courtroom and thus unable to cover the trial.

```
                UNITED STATES DISTRICT COURT
                  DISTRICT OF MASSACHUSETTS

                            )
UNITED STATES OF AMERICA    )
                            )
V.                          )        NO.   99-CR-10371-DJC
                            )
JAMES J. BULGER             )
                            )

              DEFENDANT'S AMENDED WITNESS LIST

     The defendant, James J. Bulger, submits this witness list

pursuant to the Court's Order dated March 26, 2013. ECF Dkt. No.

851. The defendant reserves the right to supplement, modify or

withdraw witnesses from this list.

     1.    Michael Albano
           Medford, MA

     2.    Earl Anderson
           Roseau, MN

     3.    Jeannette Benedetti
           Walpole, MA

     4.    Richard Bergeron
           Quincy, MA

     5.    Sam Berkowitz
           Royal Palm Beach FL 33411

     6.    Brian Burke

     7.    Howard Carr
           Brighton, MA 02135

     8.    Jerry Campbell
           Boston, MA

     9.    Neal Cherkas
           Chelsea, MA
```

Defense Witness List (author is number 7)

The judge quickly allowed the reporters in.

The jury was composed of eight men and four women, and in his opening veteran prosecutor Kelly briefly described to them the litany of charges—extortion, drug dealing, money laundering, possession of machine guns, 19 murders.

"It's about a criminal enterprise that ran amok in the City of Boston for almost 30 years," he said. "And at the center of all this murder and mayhem is one man, the defendant in this case, James Bulger.

"You will hear that eventually, while he started out as just one of many members of this enterprise, eventually he took control. He became the leader. And he was no ordinary leader. He did the dirty work himself, because he was a hands-on killer."

Then Kelly told the story of Arthur "Bucky" Barrett, murdered and interred in the basement of a South Boston home in 1983, a "crime of opportunity," as it would be called, after they stole $57,000 in cash from him.

He described one of the prosecution's future witnesses, a surly thug named Kevin Weeks, keeping guard over the doomed Charlestown burglar.

"Kevin Weeks watched him as he said his prayers."

Then Kelly struck what would be a recurring theme in the trial—Whitey's habit of taking a nap after committing a murder.

"Bulger didn't get involved in the burial process, he let his other gang members do that. He stayed upstairs and rested on the couch."

Next, another point to which the prosecution would return again and again.

"You will hear that Bulger liked to promote the myth that he had nothing to do with drugs."

Kelly briefly mentioned "public corruption"—the bribing of large numbers of law enforcement. And then he got to the charge that perhaps irritated the defendant more than any other, even though it wasn't included as a count against him, because it isn't a crime to be an informant.

"Even though, as you will hear, Bulger liked to tell people he didn't like informants, or rats as he used to call them, the evidence in this case will be that Bulger was one of the biggest informants in Boston . . . Now, this, in turn, leads us to one of the grotesque ironies of this case, because you will hear about one informant, Bulger, killing other people because those other people were suspected of being informants."

Kelly next spoke about Bulger's victims who were "in the wrong place at the wrong time"—innocent victims of Winter Hill's gangland gats.

But most of the dead, Kelly continued, Bulger meant to kill. Like Eddie Connors, a Dorchester barroom owner was "bragging too loudly and too much about helping Bulger's gang"—he didn't mention that the help Connors had provided was in setting up another, earlier victim of the gang.

"So, what happened to Eddie Connors? He was told by one of the gang members to go to a phone booth in Dorchester for an important phone call. But when he got there, there was no phone call. Instead, death came calling. Death came calling in the form of this man over here, James Bulger, who riddled that phone booth with bullets. Bulger and his sidekick, Stephen Flemmi, ran toward the phone booth and shot it up, killing Eddie Connors."

That provided the segue into the two major witnesses, Bulger's fellow hitmen, Stevie "the Rifleman" Flemmi and Johnny Martorano. Flemmi is

Eddie Connors shot dead in a phone booth, 1975

serving life plus 30 years, so Kelly went directly to the issue he knew defense attorney Carney would soon be raising—that Martorano was sentenced to a mere 14 years for 20 murders.

"Not enough," Kelly conceded. But originally "the Cook" wasn't facing any murder charges, Kelly pointed out, and that by confessing "he basically doubled his punishment. Still not enough . . . But he did confess, and he did solve crimes that had been unsolved for three decades."

Next he brought up Stevie Flemmi, Whitey's closest associate, his fellow rat, whose girlfriends Whitey was charged with murdering with his bare hands.

"Now, Flemmi and Bulger were so close that Flemmi bought a house, a house in South Boston right across from Bulger's brother's house. The houses literally face each other. Let me show you a picture of that."

This was the first mention at trial of Whitey's brother, the politician known at the State House as "the Corrupt Midget." It would not be the last.

Kelly mentioned how the "sun porch" behind Flemmi's house was where the 14 guns mentioned in the indictment, including the six machine guns, had been stashed. Kelly sketched out a couple more extortions before returning to Kevin Weeks, a loan shark and cocaine supplier who "did even more than drug dealing. He also helped—he helped bury bodies for Bulger."

The facing South Boston homes of Billy Bulger (left) and Stevie Flemmi's parents (right)

The Organizational Chart of the Winter Hill Gang

Next, a history lesson. Kelly showed a chart of the original Winter Hill Gang, in which Whitey was one of six "partners," along with Flemmi, Martorano, Howie Winter, Joe McDonald and Jimmy Sims.

Kelly pointed out that the gang's name came not from Howie Winter, the original boss of the gang, but from the Winter Hill section of Somerville. But by the early 1980's, three of the partners—Martorano, Sims and McDonald—were "on the lam," and Winter was in prison.

Only Whitey and Stevie remained in Boston, and what was now simply called "Southie" or "the Bulger group" plunged into the drug business bigtime. Kelly showed another chart, that of Whitey's 1980's drug organization.

Frank Lepere

Kelly mentioned Frank Lepere, a "giant marijuana dealer back in the 1980's." He had to pay all the time when he brought a load of marijuana into the Boston area. They also supplied him with "protection," sometimes lethal protection.

Kelly then went back to the "house of horrors" at 799 East Third Street, where Bucky Barrett and two others had been murdered by Whitey and then interred in shallow graves in the cellar. And how the bodies were eventually exhumed on Halloween night 1985 and reburied on Hallet Street in Dorchester across from Florian Hall.

Winding down, Kelly told the story of how the corrupt FBI agents on Bulger's payroll had tipped off Whitey in December 1994 to the pending indictment against him. That head start allowed Bulger to flee and hide out for 16 years until in 2011 "honest FBI agents," as Kelly described them, tracked him down. He used the word "honest" a second time when he recounted how the "honest FBI agents" found guns, fake IDs and cash, over $800,000 in cash.

Billy Bulger with John Kerry and Teresa Heinz

Billy and Ted Kennedy at "Halitosis Hall" on St. Patrick's Day in Southie

Finally, Kelly arrived at the 19 murders included in the racketeering acts, and in the most memorable visual of the trial, photos of all 19 appeared on the courthouse screen, one after another, as Kelly read their names, in chronological order of their deaths:

"You will hear about Michael Milano, Al Plummer, William O'Brien, James O'Toole, Al Notarangeli, James Sousa, Paul McGonagle, Edward Connors, Thomas King, 'Buddy' Leonard, Richard Castucci, Roger Wheeler, Debra Davis, Brian Halloran, Michael Donahue, John Callahan, 'Bucky' Barrett, John McIntyre and Deborah Hussey."

From 1972 to 1985. Thirteen years, 19 murders.

After that, Jay Carney's opening seemed anticlimactic. He talked about the FBI crusade that began in the 1960's against the Mafia, and how John "Zip" Connolly, Whitey's bought-and-paid-for fed, was regarded as "the FBI golden boy because of his ability to provide information."

Carney lowered his voice as he began to recount this cautionary tale of the law-enforcement Icarus who flew too close to the sun.

"All of this acclaim, these raises, these promotions, these awards went to his head. John Connolly thought he was a rock star, and he became greedy.

Whitey's 19 Alleged Murder Victims

Michael Milano

Al Plummer

William O'Brien

James O'Toole

Al Notarangeli

James Sousa

Paul McGonagle (on the left)

Edward Connors

Thomas King

Buddy Leonard (with wife Constance)

Richard Castucci (with Frank Sinatra)

Roger Wheeler

Debra Davis

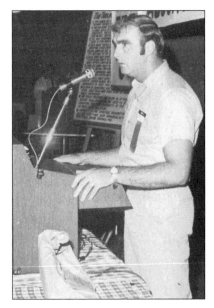

Brian Halloran

Michael Donahue

John Callahan

Bucky Barrett

John McIntyre

Deborah Hussey

"Now, James Bulger never, ever, the evidence will show, was an informant for John Connolly. There were two reasons for this. Number one, James Bulger is of Irish descent, and the worst thing that an Irish person could consider doing was becoming an informant because of the history of the troubles in Ireland. And that was the first and foremost reason why James Bulger was never an informant against people."

The name "Gypo Nolan" never came up in this or any other context during the trial. And the Bulger brother who used the fictional rat's name as such a slur on his fellow Hibernians—William M. Bulger—never once appeared in the courtroom. It was left to Jackie Bulger, himself a convicted felon (perjury, obstruction of justice) to carry the family banner.

Despite the overwhelming evidence against him, Whitey was determined to prove, or at least try to prove, that he was not an informant. After all, there aren't any rat legends in American criminal history—Joe Barboza? Joe Valachi? Sammy the Bull Gravano? Not even close.

Whitey's second aim was to convince the jury that he did not murder those "two girls," Debra Davis and Deborah Hussey. The fact that the government was prepared to produce witnesses to both murders, in addition to more than 700 pages of his informant file, did not seem to faze Carney or his client in the least.

Carney next explained that Whitey could not have provided information about the Mafia because as a non-Italian he could never be privy to In Town's secrets. In reality, he said, Connolly was Bulger's informant, with the greedy G-man taking cash "to live the lavish lifestyle, and Jim Bulger had the money to help him do so. He wasn't paid small amounts of money. James Bulger paid John Connolly on occasion $5,000, on other occasions $10,000, on still other occasions $50,000."

And so, Carney continued, making it up as he went along, "Connolly created this (informant) file just to cover up the fact that he was being seen

John Connolly in handcuffs

with Bulger so often, that he was meeting with him when Bulger would be providing him money. His file grew to hundreds of pages."

Finally, Carney came up with a reasonable question for the jury: "Ask yourselves, would an informant be paying tens of thousands of dollars to the agent? Wouldn't it be the other way around, if the agent was paying Bulger for information? That never happened."

And why did Bulger need such information? It was here that Carney's argument went off the tracks.

"He wanted information. James Bulger was involved in criminal activities in Boston. He was involved in illegal gaming—bookmaking. He also lent money to people at very high rates—it's called loan-sharking. He was involved in drug dealing. These crimes, that's what he did."

In the blink of an eye, Carney had conceded enough of the counts against his client to send him to prison for the rest of his life, even if he had been 33, not 83.

Whitey, Carney said, paid off the corrupt cops for information—about wiretaps, about bugs, when warrants were issued, where searches for contraband would be conducted and finally, if he were to be indicted, "a heads up so he could leave town. That's what he was paying for.

"This was how James Bulger was able to do illegal gambling, make illegal loans, be involved in drug trafficking and extortion of people, and never, ever be charged, and on top of that, make millions upon millions upon millions of dollars doing so."

It was an unfortunate, if memorable, choice of words—millions upon millions upon millions. People remembered it all too well. It appeared in most newspaper stories the next day, the feds mentioned it in the closing, and then used it yet again after the trial in their forfeiture motion, when they accused Bulger of amassing $25.2 million in ill-gotten gains.

As for fleeing the jurisdiction after his indictment, Carney explained with a straight face that "Mr. Bulger was driving back to Massachusetts from a brief vacation" when he heard the news on the radio that a warrant had been issued for his arrest and that Stevie Flemmi had already been lugged earlier that evening.

"The tip came from the fact that the prosecution's office had to publicize what they were doing." In order, you see, to protect the guy who paid them off and who had been granted carte blanche immunity by a mid-level federal bureaucrat.

In Plain Sight?

Whitey's Irish passport photo

Whitey's fake "National ID"

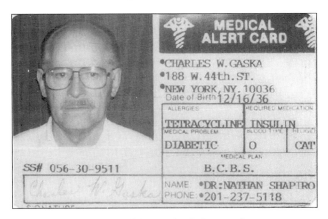

Whitey's fake Medical Alert card

Whitey's fake Social Security card

"Mr. Bulger turned around and did not drive to Massachusetts but drove elsewhere. And that's why he was not arrested in Boston. It was something as mundane as that. He settled in California, not hiding, living openly in plain sight for the next 16 years while those former FBI agents, I submit, pretended to look for him."

No objections were raised to this "total bullshit," as one juror would describe Carney's arguments after the trial ended. Opening arguments are not considered evidence. Lawyers can say almost anything you like—and Carney did, and even on the few occasions when Kelly objected, citing "accuracy," Judge Casper overruled him.

Carney's next target was Johnny Martorano. He said Martorano had learned to be a rat from his "mentor," Joe Barboza. Martorano had in fact never spoken to Barboza again after he flipped, and had offered to testify against him in the murder case where the FBI allowed Barboza's testimony to frame four innocent men. When Martorano himself was later questioned on cross-examination about his alleged plans to follow in the footsteps of "the Animal," Martorano seemed puzzled as to why anyone would think he would even consider such a poor career choice.

"He (Barboza) got killed for being an informant," Martorano pointed out.

But Carney was determined to undercut Martorano's credibility before he took the stand.

"It would be fair to say that he is the scariest criminal, violent psychopath in Boston history. He would kill people almost randomly, just as the

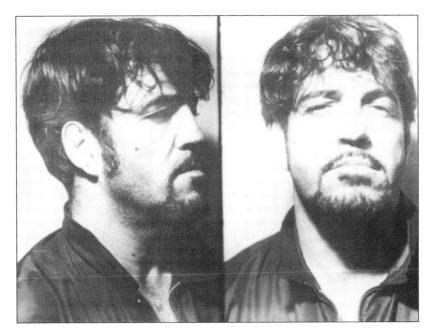

Joe Barboza

mood befit him. He would kill people because they crossed him. He would kill people because he wanted to get their money."

In other words, he sounded a lot like Carney's client.

"He would kill people as easily as we would order a cup of coffee in a store."

As for Weeks, he asked the jury, "What do you think is a fair sentence for killing five people? The prosecutors thought a total of five years . . . I submit that Kevin Weeks can't tell the truth, even when there is nothing at stake for him."

Finally, Carney reached Stevie Flemmi, the most important witness— at least to Whitey's "legacy." The two

Stevie Flemmi

Debs that Whitey claimed he didn't kill, they were Flemmi's women. In addition to being his rape victim, Deb Hussey was also Flemmi's stepdaughter. The insurmountable problem for Whitey was that both Weeks and Flemmi had seen him strangle Deb Hussey at 799 East Third Street. Two against one is prosecution fun.

In the case of Debra Davis, who was strangled at the South Boston home of Flemmi's parents on the same day Stevie closed on the property, it was Whitey's word against Stevie's.

"You heard about the death of a beautiful young woman named Debbie Davis. Stevie was much older than she was." Twenty-three years, to be exact. "He was extremely generous to her family, and he was very proud that Debbie Davis was his girlfriend. But then he learned that she was cheating on him. He learned who her paramour or secret lover was. He learned that she was mocking Stevie as being an old man, somebody who gave her money. She was going to keep taking his money.

"Well, when you're dating someone who is a psychopath without a conscience, that's the last thing that person needs to know. And Stevie Flemmi, the evidence will show, decided to kill her.

"In fact, Stevie Flemmi spoke to Martorano on one occasion, and Martorano asked, 'What happened with Debbie?' And Stevie Flemmi said, 'I strangled her.'"

Not quite. According to Martorano, Flemmi told him, "I accidentally strangled her." Martorano would testify to that, under oath, when he was recalled as a defense witness seven weeks later at the end of the trial. Flemmi, convicted of perjury in addition to 10 murders and assorted other crimes, testified he had no recollection of any such conversation.

Sometimes a lawyer has to follow his client's instructions, no matter how misguided they may seem. So despite two witnesses, Carney tried to explain in advance why Whitey would never have murdered Stevie's stepdaughter.

"When Deborah was a teenager, Stevie Flemmi was sexually abusing her, and he did for years . . . What if she told her mother? And then one day, she did tell her mother, and Flemmi was booted out of the house. Well, if she could tell her mother, what if the police found out?"

With time running out, he returned to his central, if flawed theme: that Whitey was too high up in the hood hierarchy to be committing such messy crimes.

"What the evidence will show is that Bulger is a person who had an unbelievably lucrative criminal enterprise in Boston. He was making millions and millions of dollars."

Too much money to be killing people randomly, Carney seemed to be implying.

Finally, with a simple "Thank you, your Honor," Carney sat down. In 90 minutes, he hadn't once mentioned the possibility of his client testifying. Not even a hint of it.

Two Weeks

It was July 8, the 16th day of the trial.

"The government," said prosecutor Brian Kelly, "would call Kevin Weeks."

Only now he was better known in South Boston as "Two Weeks." It was probably the smartest move Kevin Weeks ever made in the rackets—deciding to flip a mere two weeks after his arrest in November 1999. In his 2006 book, *Brutal,* he recalled a Mafia soldier he was jailed with in Rhode Island as asking him incredulously why he was "taking it up the ass" for two rats.

Kevin Weeks was obviously asking himself that same question. But not for long. Two Weeks—it wasn't complimentary, but it actually wasn't that much more derogatory than the handle he used to be known by in Southie in the glory days.

Kevin Squeaks.

Now, he was taking the stand against the man who had made him everything he had become—gangster, murderer, drug dealer, pathological liar.

Whitey and Weeks, with Yale sweatshirt

Weeks was always "the kid," 27 years younger than Whitey, 22 years Stevie's junior. But at age 57, he was no longer young. Like Whitey, he'd grown up in the projects—Old Colony, in his case. Both his brothers had gone to Harvard, but Weeks graduated from South Boston High School in 1974, the year busing started in Boston. He soon dropped out of college and began drifting from one menial job to another. He ended up working as a bouncer at Triple O's, the Bulger bar in the Lower End. The owner of record: Kevin O'Neil, another Bulger mobster who would be arrested on the same day as Weeks in 1999. Whitey watched him on the door at Triple O's, as well as breaking up fights inside the bar. He saw something in the young plug-ugly—a nasty temper, a hulking frame, and not too much upstairs. Soon Whitey and Weeks were talking all the time.

In 1980, Weeks married and did the Southie thing—he got a job at the Mass. Bay Transportation Authority, the MBTA, also known as "Mr. Bulger's Transportation Authority." Billy Bulger, not Whitey. You could collect a full pension after only 23 years. One of Whitey's nephews retired from the T at 43, another at age 45.

Had he stayed "on the T," Weeks could have retired in 2003, at age 47. Instead, he was still working in the private sector, a construction job, although once again, he'd taken the Southie way.

"I was injured on the job," he explained as prosecutor Kelly began his direct examination. "I got hit by a machine, I had two surgeries, so—"

"Sir," Kelly interrupted, "can you move that back?"

He was asking Weeks to move his microphone. Kelly didn't care about the injury, nor did anyone else in the courtroom. Another Southie guy out on workman's comp. What else was new?

This was Weeks' fifth, maybe sixth trial. He'd lost count over the years.

Kelly went over the usual preliminaries, what he'd pleaded guilty to (five murders, aiding and abetting) and his alleged literary career. After declaring bankruptcy, and being sued by some of his victims' survivors for wrongful death, he signed a book contract with Judith Regan, who would soon be fired by Rupert Murdoch for paying O.J. Simpson $3.5 million for his ill-fated memoir, *If I Did It*.

Kevin Weeks' advance was $40,000. After paying off his ghostwriter, the literary agent, and the victims' families, he ended up with about $8,000.

"Did you ever even read this book?" Kelly asked.

"No."

Now Kelly returned to his apprenticeship, as it were, in the rackets. As an MBTA trackman in the early 1980's, he had plenty of free time, which he increasingly spent with Whitey either at Triple O's or at the mob's appliance store. They grew "closer and closer." Eventually, Weeks quit the T and went to work for Whitey.

"Basically we just rode around. Sometimes I beat somebody up, but it wasn't really, you know, doing much of anything. Pick up some envelopes from bookmakers."

The Mafia underboss of Boston, Gennaro Angiulo, once famously said that, "I don't need tough guys, I need intelligent tough guys."

Whitey had a different theory. He didn't want his tough guys too intelligent. He'd seen where that led—to his old boss Donald Killeen getting shot to death in a car in Framingham in 1972, and his bar, the Transit Café, turning suddenly into Triple O's.

Weeks did have one edge over everyone else in the gang. He had no police record, which meant he could legally carry a firearm. That was his main job, that and beating people up, or at least threatening to. Whitey's work day started around 3 or 3:30, and they'd drive around, then split up to go home for dinner, "and then I'd meet him later that night."

Triple O's in the 1980's

He learned never to speak on the phone, or inside, or in the car—anyplace that could be bugged. Any serious business was conducted outside, usually on walks around Castle Island, or the "Sugar Bowl," a walkway jutting out into the harbor, or in Columbia Park.

As usual, the prosecution showed the photograph of Stevie Flemmi's parents' house on East Third Street.

"And who lived to the left?" Kelly asked, once again.

"That was Jimmy's brother, Billy." The Senate president.

Kelly ran him through various trips he'd made taking guns back and forth between "hides," always wearing gloves—"It's kind of common sense, I mean, amongst criminals."

Whitey also kept a stash of masks, brass knuckles, at least one authentic Boston Police badge, and even some handcuffs.

Gennaro Angiulo

Flemmi, Weeks and Bulger, mocking the cops by having an outdoor
"sit-down" in Columbia Park

"If we were shaking someone down," Weeks said, "sometimes they were used in murders where we would handcuff the person."

Whitey always had knives around—"intimidation," Weeks explained.

In 1982, Weeks finally made his bones. He was the lookout when Whitey murdered Brian Halloran and Michael Donahue outside the Port Café on Northern Avenue. Brian Halloran had become a rat for the FBI—and only two FBI rats were allowed in Southie. They called Halloran "Balloonhead," and when he got up from the booth he'd been drinking in all afternoon, Weeks used his two-way radio to call Whitey.

"The Balloon's rising," he said. Then, as Halloran got outside, "The Balloon's in the air."

Michael Donahue was a friend of Halloran's who was giving him a ride home. He was driving his father's little

Brian Halloran

Port Café on Northern Avenue—last call for Brian Halloran

blue Datsun, and Halloran hopped in. Then Whitey pulled up in the "tow truck," the gang's hit car, and yelled, "Brian!" Another guy, wearing a ski mask in May, was sitting in the backseat with a gun, but it jammed.

Whitey's withering fire immediately killed Donahue, but Halloran was in the passenger seat, shielded by Donahue's body, and he was only wounded. He opened the door and staggered out of the car. Weeks was watching everything.

Donahue Death Datsun

"As he walked toward the rear of his vehicle, he actually was walking right toward where Jim Bulger was parked, you know, in the street. And Jim Bulger just started shooting at him . . . Brian Halloran went down, and Jim Bulger kept on shooting him, and his body was bouncing off the ground."

Then Bulger sped off. Later he and Weeks met up, and in a different car they returned to the murder scene. As Whitey had been making his turn in the tow truck on the viaduct to escape, the hubcap had come off.

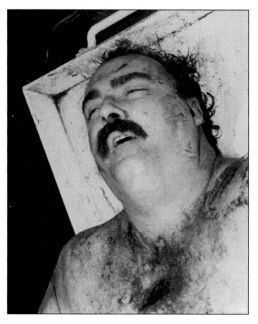

Halloran body

"So we went down the viaduct, and we could see the crime scene with the lights and everything. So we picked up the hubcap. I jumped out and grabbed the hubcap, and then we drove away."

Then they went back to Flemmi's house. Weeks sullenly watched the TV news reports, thinking, "I just was involved in a double homicide, so there was no getting out. I knew I was in."

In the kitchen, Whitey was regaling Stevie with details of the hit, and how he was "just putting them (bullets) into him." Stevie was "upset" that he'd been unavailable.

(At trial a few days later, the medical examiner would testify that Halloran's autopsy indicated 22 gunshot wounds from 14 shots, and that he had died from loss of blood. Donahue was shot four times, and the final shot was to the back of his head, which entered his brain causing instantaneous death.)

"Did Mr. Bulger make any attempt," Kelly asked, "to minimize his role?"

"No. He—it was all about him at that time."

It was all about him all the time. He was so proud of his handiwork that a couple of days later, the three of them drove over to the tow lot in

Southie where Donahue's shot-up blue Datsun was being stored. Finally, after about five minutes, Whitey said, "Let's get out of here before someone spots us."

Later, Weeks went to the garage where the tow truck was hidden. He took out the guns, but before throwing them into the ocean, he removed the stock from the carbine Whitey had used to murder Halloran and Donahue.

"He liked that stock," Weeks said.

Next Kelly guided him through some of the gang's extortions. Nobody ever refused to pay—"never really happened. I mean, they'd get hurt."

Several of the victims would soon be testifying, but this was a way to introduce them to the jury. First, Michael Solimando, the business partner of another gang murder victim, shaken down for more than $400,000 in the fall of 1982. Solimando was a body builder, in good shape, so on the second floor of Triple O's, Bulger put a machine gun to his crotch.

"He said, 'Your muscles ain't gonna do you any good now.'"

Kelly asked if Solimando and his partners really owed Whitey $400,000.

"No. It was a crime of opportunity. It was—you know, it was BS."

Weeks' cut was $80,000.

Next was Richard Buccheri, another future witness. He was a developer, a friend of the Martoranos. Weeks had just bought a house in Quincy, and discovered that his neighbor's fence was six inches onto his property. The new neighbor asked Weeks to cut him some slack, but Weeks told him the bank insisted the fence had to go.

So the neighbor went to Buccheri and asked for his advice. Buccheri told him to go to the seller and get him to backdate the deed, making the fence legal. Perhaps knowing who he was dealing with, the seller instead went to Weeks, who went to Bulger. Buccheri was summoned to the sun porch. When he emerged, Weeks recounted, "He was white. He was shaking."

Buccheri paid $200,000. Weeks got $50,000.

Ray Slinger was an insurance salesman. He had a beef with Kevin O'Neil, so he was brought up to the second floor of Triple O's. He was wearing a long coat, which Weeks noticed he was wearing to hide a gun in his waistband. Weeks relieved him of the weapon, and handed it to Bulger, who gave Slinger a vicious kick in the shin as he stood on some tarp that had been laid down on the floor.

"Jim Bulger told him, 'I can kill you now, shoot you in the head, top of the head. There will be no blood. No one will ever know.' He was—Slinger was scared, and then we told him—Jim Bulger told him that, you know, he's been offered money to kill him."

More BS. Slinger was told he now owed them $50,000. He paid $25,000 but after he went to the FBI O'Neil went down to his office and told him to forget about the rest.

Next was Kevin Hayes, a City Hall hack and a wannabe bookie. One day in 1994 he went into one of their stores, Rotary Variety. Kevin Weeks was behind the counter. Hayes struck up a conversation and was soon bragging to Weeks about his four or five bookies, and how if Weeks ever wanted to place a bet, he should call him. Then Hayes asked what his name was.

"I said 'Kevin Weeks' and the color went out of him. I looked at him and said, 'Yeah, you never know who you're talking to.'"

Hayes was eventually brought to the home of Pat Nee—the Matterhorn, they called it. Nee was in prison on an armored-car beef, so they had the place to themselves. Weeks didn't go into great detail about this shakedown, but on the stand a week later, the 57-year-old Hayes recounted everything.

He was brought to the Matterhorn by Patty Linskey and a newcomer named John McMurray. This time it was Weeks reprising the role of his mentor, right down to the tarp. Hayes recalled Weeks' pitch very well.

"He said, 'You MF'er, you disrespect us. We should just kill you right now. That's why the plastic is laid out, so when we blow your brains out we clean it up easy."

Meanwhile, an unidentified gangster was pacing back and forth.

"He was just saying, 'Just put a cap in his head.'"

Hayes couldn't even remember how much he was shaken down for—$10,000 or $20,000. He delivered it the next day to McMurray at the Orange Line stop at North Station. Soon thereafter, he was out of business—"I told them I wasn't making any money."

Just Weeks' luck—shaking down a bookie who was going broke.

Kelly spent more time on the earlier, more profitable "crimes of

Stippo Rakes

opportunity." Like stealing Stippo Rakes' liquor store. Although Weeks claimed that was actually a business transaction. Stippo's sister, one of the gang's drug dealers, had gone to another of their bars, at F and Second Streets, and said Stippo was getting death threats at his new liquor store. The other package store owners in Southie hated Stippo—he had a great location on Old Colony Ave., between the projects, and he had free parking.

Then almost by accident Whitey found out who was making the threats—an old bookie in Andrew Square who now owned a bar and package store. He was bragging to Whitey that he wanted Stippo to have some "sleepless nights." Whitey told him to knock it off and the calls stopped.

Still, Stippo wanted to sell, or so Weeks said. They offered him $100,000, and Stippo accepted the deal. Whitey put in $70,000 cash and Weeks came up with $30,000. They put the money in a paper bag and went up to Stippo's house. His little daughter was toddling around the kitchen. She climbed onto Whitey's lap, as Weeks recalled.

"And Stippo started talking, and he goes: 'Well, you know, my wife, I don't think—she don't want to sell now. You know, the money. I mean, it's worth more and stuff.' He was trying to shake us down. We had an agreement with him for the 100,000, and now, all of a sudden, at the last minute, he's backing out and he's blaming his wife for it. He was looking to shake us down, and that wasn't going to happen. So I pulled a gun out. I had it in my waistband. I put it on the table and I said, 'Stippo, we had a deal.' And then the little girl that was on Jim Bulger's lap, she reached for the gun."

Whitey told Weeks to put away the gun. He took over the "negotiations," saying, "You ain't backing out." Stippo didn't back out.

Kelly asked, "But he was forced to sell when you pulled out the gun?"

"You know," Weeks began, "yeah, he was forced, but, I mean, we didn't go to him to buy the store. He came to us. It wasn't your regular extortion."

Kelly kept going over the extortions—$500,000 from Joe Murray, the Charlestown drug dealer, when he wanted out of his "partnership" with Whitey. They called that shakedown "severance." Murray delivered it the next day to Weeks and Nee at the Aquarium in a big black duffle bag he handed out the window of his car.

It was a small price to pay for escaping the clutches of Whitey, who by this time had already murdered at least two members of Murray's crew. As the primary go-between to fellow Irish freedom sympathizer Murray,

Nee got $125,000. Weeks, Whitey and Stevie each took $90,000, and the remaining $105,000 went into the "X" fund. "X" as in "expenses."

Hobart Willis was another Southie/Dorchester cocaine dealer ripe for the picking. He had a big mouth.

"He was using derogatory terms for the Mafia, the Italians, basically calling them 'guineas.' And they found out. And Jimmy went to him and told him that they were going to kill him, and Hobart Willis ended up paying $250,000."

Hobart Willis, another "rent-paying" Southie drug dealer

"For what?" asked Kelly.

"Not to get killed," replied Weeks.

Anybody who sold cocaine in Southie had to pay. They found out about a guy named Jack Cherry.

"He was dealing drugs and we found out about it." The three of them—Weeks, Whitey and Stevie—drove to his house on Fourth Street. "Jim and Stevie went inside and told Jackie Cherry that they had been offered $50,000 to kill him, that he had sold drugs to a young kid, and the grandfather was upset and was offering money to kill him."

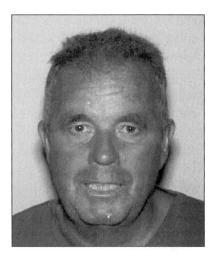

Jack Cherry—another victim of a gang "ruse"

KELLY: "Was that true?"

WEEKS: "No."

Then there was Anthony Attardo, another drug dealer whose doings Whitey often reported to Zip Connolly. He was shaken down for $65,000.

"His brother got shot in the stomach in Dorchester and—from some kids over in Charlestown. And we told him they were looking to kill his brother, and that we would intervene on his behalf, but we weren't going to do it for nothing. So he paid us $65,000 to make sure his brother didn't get killed."

KELLY: "Was that a phony story, too?"

WEEKS: "Yeah. Well, the shooting wasn't, but what we were going to do, yes."

A few days later Attardo would tell a different version of the story, starting with the fact that he said he paid $80,000 in extortion, not $65,000. According to Attardo, he was moving

Anthony Attardo—paid $80,000

25 kilos a month, which he bought from Colombians in Miami. At one point he bought a single kilo from Patty Linskey "just to keep the heat off." Not only was the price exorbitant—$44,000—but the coke "was lousy. It was no good."

Attardo refused to buy any more from Whitey's organization, so he was called down to the liquor store—this was 1985 or 1986, and what had once been Stippo's was now renamed the South Boston Liquor Mart, complete with a giant green shamrock painted on its wall. The Liquor Mart was slowly supplanting Triple O's as the gang's headquarters, just as Triple O's had replaced the appliance store and the old Mullens gang clubhouse on O Street.

At the package store, Whitey went into his usual routine with Attardo.

"He says to me, 'I heard you're moving a lot of cocaine.' He goes to me, 'I never bothered you. I never asked you for nothing. I want $100.000.' And I told him I'm not doing nothing no more. I'm out of business. He said, 'Don't lie to me. The money is so good, the only time you're going to quit is when you are going to jail.' He was right about that."

After Whitey fled, Attardo heard about some Dominican drug dealers making big money and "I decided maybe we should maybe pull a 'Whitey' Bulger and extort them."

The "Dominicans" turned out to be undercover cops.

Prosecutor Zach Hafer asked him, "So that didn't work out too well?"

ATTARDO: "No, it didn't."

He did eight years for that, and for trying to buy $30,000 worth of Percocets from yet another undercover police officer.

But in the 1980's, Attardo was on top of his game as a cocaine dealer. When Whitey told him "something was going to happen" if he didn't pay, he decided to do something about it. He went across the bridge into the South End and talked to a relative of Mafia boss Larry Zannino, Sonny Baione, at his tavern with the Narragansett Beer sign out front. In other words, Attardo was seeking assistance from In Town.

"I said, 'Can you help me out and maybe talk to Mr. Bulger?' He told me the best thing to do, if you have the money, pay him, because he—that's his neighborhood. That's his town. You can't control him."

In other words, In Town was giving Whitey a pass. They had their hands full with other headaches, many of which involved investigations instigated by Whitey and his corrupt cadre of FBI agents.

Open under New Management—South Boston Liquor Mart, formerly known as Stippo's

Attardo went back to Southie and became very careful. But he came from a big family, and soon his 17-year-old brother was shot and wounded in Charlestown.

"After he got shot, Mr. Bulger with Kevin Weeks came to my house. He knocked on my door. I opened it. Mr. Bulger says, 'You're next if you don't give money.' And I said, 'I'll meet you down the liquor store.'"

HAFER: "Did you think he shot your brother?"

ATTARDO: "Yes, of course. Yes."

HAFER: "What was Mr. Bulger's reputation?"

ATTARDO: "Very dangerous. He meant what he said."

HAFER: "Mr. Attardo, in all the years you dealt cocaine in South Boston, did you ever know 'Whitey' Bulger to be involved in trying to keep cocaine out of South Boston?"

ATTARDO: "That was a rumor. If it was true, I don't know."

3

"You Suck!"

Weeks' second day on the witness stand, July 9, would be the most emotional day of the entire trial. Most of his testimony involved the murders he'd been involved in, and he was going over familiar ground from earlier trials. But Whitey had been on the lam during those proceedings, so it was all new to him, listening to his "surrogate son," as he described Weeks to extortion victim Buccheri, tie him to one grisly slaying after another.

And it would finally drive Whitey over the edge.

Under the brisk questioning of Kelly, Weeks began with the murder of Arthur "Bucky" Barrett, the Charlestown burglar who was the architect of the monumental Depositors Trust bank burglary in Medford over Memorial Day weekend in 1980.

Kevin Weeks' least favorite mugshot

Bucky Barrett's last driver's license

The gang had tried to shake Barrett down earlier, with another "ruse"—falsely claiming that imprisoned Winter Hill boss Howie Winter had a safe-deposit box that was looted. Then Zip Connolly was sent over to tell Barrett he was on Whitey's radar screen. But Bucky didn't panic, he just drove to MCI-Norfolk to visit Flemmi's imprisoned partner (and future Mafia boss) Cadillac Frank Salemme. Salemme, who had grown to despise Stevie and Whitey as "jackals," told them to back off. They backed off.

But a couple of years later, Weeks and Whitey were headed to a travel agency in Dorchester where Bulger was going to make some vacation plans. Going up the stairs, they saw Bucky Barrett coming down. He said he'd been visiting his "P.O."—his probation officer. They exchanged some small talk and went on their

Salemme after prison release

respective ways, but it was a fateful encounter for Bucky, a fatal encounter as it turned out.

"After that," Weeks said, "Jimmy got interested in Bucky again."

Pat Nee's brother Michael was out of state, so the gang decided to use his house at 799 East Third Street for the shakedown. Jimmy Martorano, Johnny's younger brother, approached Bucky and told him that Kevin Weeks was selling stolen diamonds. Bucky always had a thing for hot gems. Martorano opened the door to the house and Barrett walked in, not suspecting a thing as Weeks stepped forward.

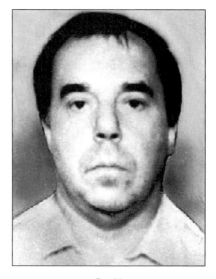

Pat Nee

"We shook hands, and I grabbed him by the hand and held him, and Jim Bulger stepped out from the kitchen with the Mac-10 nine-millimeter. He said, 'Bucky Barrett, freeze!' He then took possession of him. Stevie chained and manacled him to a chair."

Martorano quickly left, and Whitey and Stevie, mostly Whitey, began giving Bucky the rubber-hose treatment. They berated him for going to Salemme, they asked him about Murray's drug business. Even though they were now the Charlestown drug dealer's ostensible "partners," Whitey continued dreaming of a mega-score on the fabulously wealthy drug dealer.

Then they had Bucky call his wife, Elaine, who was home with two babies and no car. She later recalled her husband sounded like he was in an echo

Jimmy Martorano

chamber; in fact they'd put him on a speaker phone, so they could hear both sides of the conversation.

"In case he said something, you know, it was a code, in case she panicked. We just wanted to be ready."

Without trying to alarm her, Bucky told his wife maybe she should get someone to go out to dinner with her and the kids. He wanted her out of the house so that Whitey could pick up the $47,000 cash he had stashed there.

Finally she left, and Whitey and Stevie drove out to get the cash. They left Weeks and Nee to guard Barrett. He spent his time chained to the chair, praying.

After they returned with the $47,000, Weeks was told to go down to Barrett's bar, Little Rascals, and ask for Jake Rooney, who would give them another $10,000 in cash. Weeks first drove to the Ho Toy Chinese takeout restaurant on Old Colony Boulevard and picked up a friend of the gang named Barry Wong.

Weeks drove to Little Rascals on Broad Street in the financial district and told Wong to go in and ask for Jake, who would give him a bag. It was an old Winter Hill trick for picking up cash, using guys who would be hard to identify, if it ever came to that. Usually they sent in cabbies. In this case, a Chinese guy would work just as well.

Wong knew better than to ask questions. He walked in, picked up the bag and walked back to the car. He handed the bag to Weeks. On the witness stand a couple of days later, Wong would explain what happened next.

"Ah, next, he, ah, drove me back to the restaurant, dropped me off, and then he put out a couple of hundred-dollar bills. And I said nah, nah, nah, I don't want that. I don't need that. All right. So then I thought, what the hell, 200 is 200, so I took it."

Back at 799 East Third Street, Bucky was having a disagreement—he was in no position to have an argument—with

Joe Murray

Whitey. Bucky wanted to call Mick Murray, Joe's brother, to ask him for more money. He was the weak link, Bucky insisted. But Whitey told him to call the boss, Joe Murray.

"He basically told Joe Murray that he was going to take off, he had problems and he needed money, and if Joe didn't give it to him that he was going to give everybody up. Joe Murray swore at him and said, 'You were always a rat, go ahead.' And we didn't get any money out of him."

Weeks then left to get something to eat. While he was gone Bucky called his wife for what would be the final time.

"He said he wouldn't be home for awhile because he had to get some money," said Elaine Barrett, now 63.

Whitey beeped Weeks to return to the house. When he came back, Bulger stood Bucky up.

"He said, 'Bucky's going to go downstairs and lay down for a while.'"

Stevie went down the stairs to the basement first, with Bucky following behind, struggling with the chains. Whitey put the Mac-10 to the back of his head, not quite touching it, and pulled the trigger. Nothing.

"Then he took his glasses out," Weeks said, "put them on, he looked, the safety was on the gun. So he flicked it. Bucky had taken a couple more steps, then he just went down and shot him in the back of the head."

Bucky's body tumbled down the stairs, knocking over Flemmi, who was irate about Whitey's disregard for his safety.

Two weeks later, under questioning by prosecutor Fred Wyshak, Flemmi still seemed angry, 30 years later, about his partner's carelessness.

"I didn't know he was going to shoot Bucky, because I

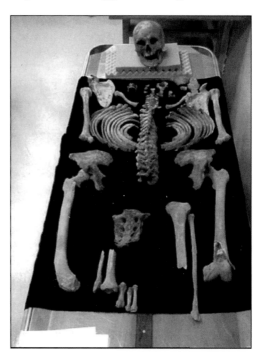

Bucky's skeleton

was right in the line of fire, and when he shot him, the bullet could have went through him and hit me, but the gun happened to be on single shot. If it was on fully automatic weapon, it would have hit me also. I said, you could have shot me."

WYSHAK: "What did he say?"

FLEMMI: "He made some asinine statement. I don't remember what it was."

Flemmi repeated that he had no idea Bucky was going to be murdered.

"He didn't have to kill him. Bucky Barrett was never going to say anything. He would have taken his loss. He was a wiseguy. He could have went out and made money on the next score. There was no reason for him to kill him. Bucky Barrett never would have said anything."

On what Whitey did next, Flemmi and Weeks agreed.

FLEMMI: "He went upstairs, lied down . . . Maybe he was mentally, physically exhausted. I don't know. Maybe he got a high on it or something and he was exhausted. That's my interpretation. It would happen at other times."

WEEKS: "He went upstairs and laid down on the couch while we took care of the cleanup."

Flemmi told Weeks to fill up a plastic bucket with cold water and then he put soap in it.

"He explained to me," Weeks recalled, "that the cold water helps congeal the blood and everything, it's easier for the cleanup, kind of teaching as he went."

Stevie Flemmi, educator. Not to mention, dentist. Because after the cleanup was completed, he began extracting Bucky's teeth—"at his (Whitey's) insistence," Flemmi insisted.

In his testimony, Flemmi said he hated his job of pulling teeth, although he just happened to have a pair of dental pliers with him, which had been obtained by Whitey's girlfriend, dental hygienist Catherine Greig. In those pre-DNA days, Flemmi considered it a foolproof way to foil later identification of the body. He'd learned his lesson back in 1969, when he'd murdered fellow Roxbury gangster Peter Poulos in the Nevada desert—another slaying he claimed he didn't want to commit, but was forced to do by Larry Baione, who considered him a weak link in the murders of the Bennett brothers.

Flemmi had made sure to strip every identifying mark off Poulos' clothes, but he neglected the teeth. A routine check of missing persons' dental records turned up Poulos' identity. The murder charges in Nevada had hung over Stevie's head for decades.

Despite Flemmi's stated misgivings, Whitey obviously thought he enjoyed the gruesome task. One of Whitey's

Dental hygienist Catherine Greig

nicknames for Flemmi was "Dr. Mengele," one of Whitey's favorite Nazis, the "Angel of Death" at the Auschwitz concentration camp during World War II (and another fugitive who'd eluded capture until his death in 1979).

As Flemmi pulled Bucky's teeth, Weeks began digging a hole. Nee returned and "was a little upset" that his brother's house had been designated

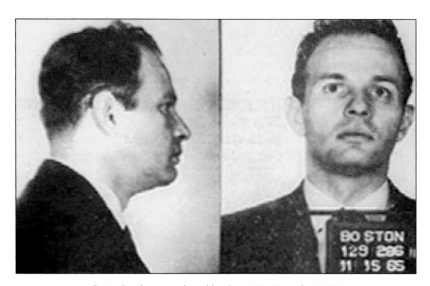

Peter Poulos, murdered by Stevie in Nevada, 1969

for use as a Mob burial ground. But once he went to work with Weeks digging the hole, Nee's anger turned to fear.

"He said, I feel like I'm digging my own hole. I said what do you want to do? He said there's nothing we can do, they got the guns."

Then came a knock on the bulkhead. It was one of Stevie's guys, Phil Costa from the Marconi Club in Roxbury. He had two bags of lime—to hasten the decomposition of the body. Very convenient, that Stevie just happened to have some lime lying around for a murder that he claimed surprise over.

By this time, Whitey had awakened from his nap. He came downstairs to view Bucky's remains one final time before the lime was poured over his corpse. Around his neck, he noticed a gold chain with a gold cross around it.

"Jim Bulger took it off him. He asked me if I wanted it. I said no. And, you know, we divided up the money that we got there. It was 57 total, that was it."

Flemmi would later be asked whether it was risky to bury a body in a house that didn't belong to you.

"I would say so," he agreed.

Phil Costa, lime man

John McIntyre

THE HOUSE would next be used in the fall of 1984, for another Murray associate. This time it was John McIntyre, a 32-year-old alcoholic from Quincy. He was the engineer on the *Valhalla*, a boat Whitey and Murray and other Irish Republican Army sympathizers had loaded with weapons to be sent to Eire. Even Stevie's brother, the crooked Boston cop Michael Flemmi, had made a donation—his BPD-issued bulletproof vest.

The ill-fated gun-running ship

The *Valhalla* made it to the rendezvous point with the Irish pick-up ship, the *Marita Anne*. But on its way back to port, the *Marita Anne* was intercepted by Irish authorities. The *Valhalla* returned to Boston and was seized by Customs. A few days later, McIntyre was arrested for drunk driving in Quincy, and he began telling the Quincy police, and later the DEA, about "the two guys who ride around together." His Quincy handler was Det. Dick Bergeron. Years later, Whitey would use one of Zip Connolly's FBI-209 reports to falsely accuse Bergeron of providing protection to a murderous crew of Quincy thugs. That was his way of getting back at Bergeron.

Under questioning from Bergeron, and later DEA agents, McIntyre mentioned that his boss, Murray, had another ship coming in, the *Ramsland*.

The *Ramsland* was much more important to Whitey Bulger than the *Valhalla*. It was carrying 36 tons of Joe Murray's marijuana, and Whitey's cut for protection, i.e., not calling the cops, was to be $1 million.

The prosecutors later brought in a retired U.S. Customs Service agent named Dennis DeFago to explain Murray's smuggling scheme. As the *Ramsland* neared Boston Harbor in November 1984, the captain told a harbor pilot that his services were not required. The *Ramsland* "sat there" for awhile, until Customs finally decided to board it.

The *Ramsland,* carrying 36 tons of marijuana

DEFAGO: "I determined that the last registry of the ship was in Norway, but that the registry had expired, that the vessel had listed as its home port under that name as London and that she was flying a British flag, but there was no British registry papers. I asked the captain who owned the vessel, and he told me it was owned by the Rio Amazonas Caribbean location, which he claimed was located in Panama."

PROSECUTOR KELLY: "Did all these things make you suspicious, sir?"

DEFAGO: "Very suspicious."

Customs decided to search the *Ramsland.* It was loaded with "literally tons" of gravel. But a Customs detector dog homed in on a certain area on the starboard side and began pawing in the gravel.

"So it was an immense job to offload it," DeFago said. "We had to bring her into port, contract a company with cranes and bobcats to move this gravel, and when we got down to it, we found that the hatch covers were cemented shut. So we had to jackhammer the hatch covers open. At a certain point in time, we discovered some marijuana."

Whitey was apoplectic. He was angrier than Murray, perhaps because Murray had so much more money; the *Ramsland* had been shaping up as

Whitey's biggest score ever. But then Zip Connolly once again came through with some information—one of the crew members from the *Valhalla* was cooperating. The Quincy police and the DEA had allowed an FBI agent to attend their interrogations of McIntyre. He was a friend of Connolly's. Maybe there was a connection to the *Ramsland* rat.

McIntyre was the logical suspect. The other crew member, the captain, was "old school," from Maine, he just didn't fit the profile. Pat Nee, who had met McIntyre during the *Valhalla* operation, was dispatched to find him. Nee told him they were putting together another marijuana deal, and offered him a chance to invest $20,000. McIntyre got the money from the DEA and handed it over to Nee. The next day Nee invited him to a "party" in Southie. Since McIntyre had lost his driver's license, Nee picked him up and drove him to 799 East Third Street in Southie. Nee walked in first, carrying a case of beer, and McIntyre followed, carrying another case.

Same routine as with Bucky Barrett: Weeks grabbed him by the neck and threw him to the ground, and Bulger stepped out of the shadows with a machine gun. Then he was chained to a chair. Pat Nee left—"he did have a party to go to," Weeks testified, "so he left."

McIntyre quickly admitted everything. He didn't know about the *Valhalla*, but he had given up the *Ramsland*.

At that point, his fate was sealed, even if McIntyre didn't know it. Whitey began questioning him, again following the Barrett script, about Joe Murray's operations, how many boats he brought in, who was in the gang, the offloading procedures, etc.

KELLY: "What as the point of asking him so many questions?

WEEKS: "Looking for the next score."

KELLY: "What does that mean?"

WEEKS: "Next person we were going to rob, shake down."

Then he was taken downstairs. Whitey took out a rope and began strangling him, but the rope was too thick.

WEEKS: "All it did was gag him. He started vomiting and stuff. And then Jim says to him, 'Do you want one in the head?' The kid

said, 'Yes, please,' and
he shot him in the back
of the head. He fell
out of the chair, kind
of hopped out of the
chair on the ground.
Then Stevie grabbed
him by the shoulder
and stuff, dragged
him over a little ways,
put his head on his
chest and said, 'He's
still alive.' And then
Jim Bulger turned
around and shot him
four, five more times,
up in the face area,
whatever, and he said,
'He's dead now.' And
then the same proce-
dure, you know, Stevie pulled
his teeth and I dig the hole and
stuff and we buried him."

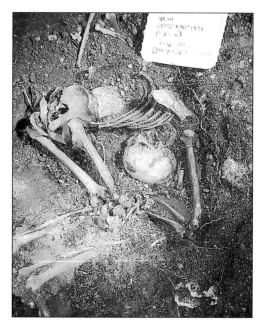

John McIntyre's remains

And Whitey took another nap.

A few months later, Weeks and
Whitey returned to the house at 799
East Third Street. Whitey told Weeks
Stevie was buying his stepdaughter,
Debbie Hussey, a coat, after which
they'd be stopping by.

"I never liked the house after people started getting killed in it," Weeks
testified, "so I was kind of relieved
when I heard Stevie was coming by
with his stepdaughter."

Deb Hussey

KELLY: "Why were you relieved?"

"You never know," Weeks replied. "It could have been my time."

> KELLY: "Why were you relieved when you were told he was coming by with his stepdaughter?"
>
> WEEKS: "It was a girl."
>
> KELLY: "Meaning what?"
>
> WEEKS: "It was a girl. It's, you know—she wasn't a criminal. She wasn't involved with us or anything I knew of in any crimes. So I didn't think anything was going to come of it."

Weeks was upstairs in the bathroom when Stevie and Debbie arrived. The next thing he heard was a thud. Whitey had the 26-year-old woman on the floor, choking her. It only took a few minutes.

"Her eyes had rolled up and her lips were blue and everything. Next, Stevie put his head on her heart. He said, 'She's still alive.' And then Stevie wrapped a rope around her neck, put a stick through it and started twisting it."

Once she was dead, they went into what had become the usual routine. Dr. Mengele on the teeth, Weeks on the hole, Whitey on the couch.

A few months later, the gang got some disconcerting news. Pat Nee's brother had decided to sell the house. They had two choices: they could buy the house, or they could move the bodies. They chose the latter solution; it was cheaper. Stevie, Weeks and Nee were in charge of digging up the bodies. The stench was overpowering. Some flesh was still clinging to Hussey's bones; she'd been in the ground less than a year. They sifted through the dirt to make sure they had picked up all the smaller bones.

The bodies, skeletons actually, were loaded into an old station wagon. Bulger was driving, with Weeks and Flemmi in the car. Nee was dismissed.

"Jimmy never really trusted Pat," Weeks said. "I don't think he wanted him to know where the bodies were."

They drove to a field on Hallet Street, across from Florian Hall, the firefighters' union headquarters and a function hall. A new hole had been dug the day before. Stevie and Whitey handled the transfer of the bodies to the hole as Weeks stood guard with a grease gun. There was one tense moment when a car pulled onto the lot. The three killers dropped to the ground and watched as a kid got out of the car and took a leak, after which he drove off. Whitey ran over to Weeks and grabbed the gun from him.

"He was upset. He told me I should have shot him, we had plenty of room in the hole, you know, basically I let him get too close."

Next Kelly ran through a number of murders that Nee had not been present for, but that Whitey had told him about.

Paul McGonagle, former Mullen murdered in 1974. "He told me he was giving Paulie McGonagle what Paulie thought was phony money, but it was actually real money, it was new bills, and he told him, see if you can move these. Naturally he could pass them because they were real money." McGonagle asked for more, and one night Whitey handed him a suitcase full of telephone books. When he opened the suitcase, Whitey shot him. He was buried on Tenean Beach in Dorchester. When Whitey and Weeks would be walking the beach, "he used to say things like, 'Drink up Paulie.'"

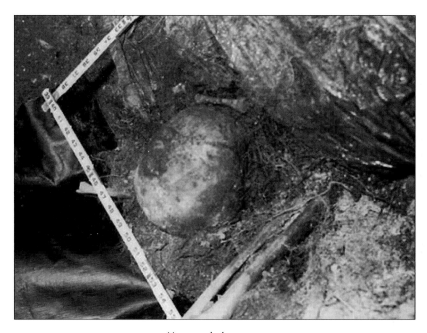

Hussey skeleton

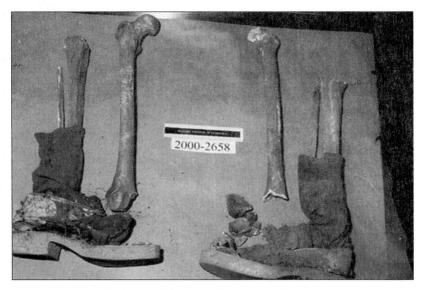

McGonagle's heels, with bones coming out

Bulger was also amused that McGonagle "had on black high heels, high shoes."

Earlier in the trial, Paul McGonagle, Jr., now 53 and an insurance broker in Virginia, had been called as a witness. He had last seen his father in November 1974, when he dropped his younger brother off at the Murphy Rink in Southie.

"My dad always told me to try to take care of my mom and brother if anything were to happen."

A year later, young McGonagle was walking down O Street. All of Southie was abuzz about the previous evening's crimes. Buddy Leonard, another former Mullen, had been found shot 13 times in a car belonging to yet another Mullen, Tommy King. The car had been left on the street Weeks lived on, Pilsudski Way. Whitey had, of course, murdered both of them, burying King as he'd buried McGonagle, after which he falsely reported to Zip Connolly that King had murdered his old pal and then fled.

Young McGonagle knew both the deceased Leonard and the "missing" King as good friends of his father. As he walked, suddenly he saw Whitey's blue Malibu pull up beside him.

"He rolled up on me with his aviator sunglasses on and told me that they had taken care of the guys that did what they did to my dad."

SPIKE O'TOOLE, former member of the McLaughlin gang, murdered outside Bulldogs Tavern on Savin Hill Avenue in December 1973. "He told me that Spike was using the mailbox as a shield, actually moving it when they were shooting at him and stuff, and that Joe McDonald got out of the car, walked over and shot him."

Debra Davis, Stevie's girlfriend, murdered in the Flemmis' house, 1981. "She was in a chair. He said when Stevie started wrapping duct tape around her face and around her hair, he said, I knew then she was gone. And he said Stevie gave her a kiss on

Bulldogs: Last call for Spike O'Toole

her forehead and said, 'You're going to a better place,' and then she was strangled. He didn't say he strangled her, he didn't say Stevie strangled her, he said, Then she was strangled, so I don't know who strangled her."

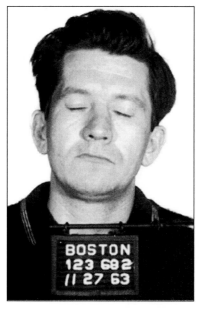

Spike O'Toole

Mailbox Spike hid behind

Now it was Jay Carney's turn to cross-examine Weeks. From the start, he seemed determined to get under Weeks' thin skin. But he started slowly. Carney asked him if Whitey was his teacher, his mentor. Weeks agreed. But not his father—"No, no, I had a father."

"How did Whitey treat you, Mr. Weeks?"

"He treated me great."

Carney asked him if Whitey had taught him how to "comport" himself as a person. Weeks agreed he had.

"Well, he showed me how to act. I mean, if you look formidable, you're less likely to have trouble with people. He also wanted me to stay out of bars so I didn't get into fights and get in trouble. It wasn't all criminal activity he taught me."

Deb Davis, in modeling photo

And it was a good-paying gig. In the course of 15 years, Weeks said he made "over a million, maybe two million." Tax free.

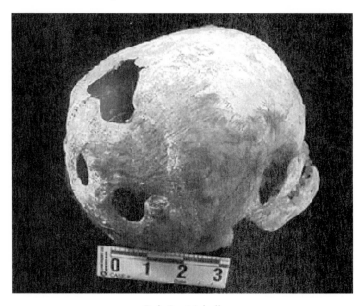

Deb Davis' skull

CARNEY: "You learned that what he hated above all else was informants, didn't you?"

WEEKS: "We killed people for being informants."

CARNEY: "In fact, you and he called them 'rats,' right?"

WEEKS: "It wasn't just us, I mean, everybody in Boston—you don't rat on your friends, you don't rat on your enemies. If you have a problem, you take it to the street and deal with it."

Eventually, Carney got around to the alleged plans by Weeks and Whitey to kill the author of this book.

CARNEY: "You hated what he was writing?"

WEEKS: "Jim Bulger did too. We went out to his house."

CARNEY: "You learned where his house was?"

WEEKS: "Ninety-nine Concord Road, yeah. Acton."

At the time, Weeks' brother Bill was a selectman in Acton.

CARNEY: "You learned what street it was on?"

WEEKS: "I just gave it to you—99 Concord Road."

Howie Carr behind Billy Bulger at U.S. House hearing in D.C. 2003

Actually, the author lived at 91 Concord Road. If Weeks had shot someone coming out of 99 Concord Road, he would have killed the wrong guy. Assuming, of course, that his story was true. The author's house was across the street from a cemetery.

"I know what the graveyard looked like. I know what my sight looked like when I was looking at him when he came out with his daughter . . . That was when I was going to shoot him. Originally, Jim Bulger wanted to put a basketball with C-4 in the driveway and blow it up when he came out."

CARNEY: "But you decided it would be better to shoot him?"

WEEKS: "No, I didn't decide. Jim Bulger—I took a rifle."

CARNEY: "Were you going to aim to kill him?"

WEEKS: "Of course I was."

CARNEY: "Now, this information you obtained allowed you to know exactly what house to go to; isn't that right?"

WEEKS: "I just told you I was out there."

Weeks was beginning to show some signs of exasperation.

CARNEY: "And then you backed off?"

WEEKS: "He come out with his daughter."

Next, Carney instructed Weeks to handle some of the weapons that had been brought into the courtroom. He started with an M-16.

CARNEY: "When you fired a gun like that, how would you hold it?"

WEEKS: "I didn't fire this gun."

CARNEY: "What is the largest clip that you had?"

WEEKS: "I didn't have a clip."

CARNEY: "Did you have these guns hidden at some point?"

WEEKS: "It's not my gun."

Next, Carney began asking about Weeks' decision in 1999 to cut a deal.

"I was worried about what Stevie was going to do," he said. "What was Stevie's next deal? He only had me and Jimmy to give up. So I made a deal before Stevie did."

Now Carney really started giving Weeks the needle. He mentioned his hated nickname, Two Weeks.

Jay Carney

CARNEY: "Now, it took you about two weeks."

WEEKS: "Did it really?"

CARNEY: "Or three weeks?

WEEKS: "How about over two years of listening to Stevie on the phone and wondering what he's going to do, and finding out that the guys I trusted the most were informants?"

CARNEY: "Mr. Weeks, it took you about two weeks after you were arrested to decide you were going to cooperate. That would be the best thing for you to do, right?"

WEEKS: "I think it was a little bit longer than that, but you can say what you want."

CARNEY: "Would three weeks be better?"

WEEKS: "I don't know. I don't know the dates. I think actually I entered it December 21. I was arrested on November 17."

So then his moniker should be Kevin "Almost Five" Weeks?

Then Carney asked him if he ever lied? He hemmed and hawed, then admitted that he hadn't told the whole truth about extorting the liquor store from Stippo Rakes.

"I've been lying my whole life," Weeks acknowledged. "I'm a criminal."

For a moment Carney let the lies . . . lie. He asked Weeks if he'd agreed to testify against his mentor, his teacher, his educator, because he thought Whitey would never be caught.

"That's not what I thought. I thought—I was hoping he would never be caught so he wouldn't be in this circus right now."

CARNEY: "The last time you met with Jim Bulger, he told you that, 'If anything comes down on you—"

WEEKS: "Put it on him."

CARNEY: "That way you could have a clear conscience—"

WEEKS: "Clear conscience? You've got a strange interpretation. Do you think this is—you know, being up here testifying against a friend, someone that I knew, that treated me well, you think that, you know, I have a clear conscience about this?"

Was Weeks worried about going to prison and being labeled a rat? No, he said, but "I was concerned that I was going to get lumped in with them as an informant. That was my real concern."

Now, Weeks said, puffing out his chest a little bit, nobody calls him a rat. "Maybe they don't have the balls to say it to my face. They might say it behind my back, but no one's ever said it to me."

If anybody did call him a rat, Weeks said, seething now, they'd have a problem. A physical problem.

"What would you do?" Carney asked him.

"Well, why don't you call me outside when it's just me and you and see what I do."

Carney now came back to the lies, asking him to elaborate on his statement about lying all his life.

"I said, 'I'm a criminal and I lie.' We all lie. All criminals lie. That's why we're criminals, you know. I'm not going to tell the truth to law enforcement if they come up and ask me something, you know, 'Do you know who did this?' or 'Did you do that?'"

Carney asked Weeks who he'd lied to.

"I lied to my parents. I lied to my wife. I lie to girlfriends."

CARNEY: "What lies do you tell your wife?"

WEEKS: "'I'm not cheating.'"

CARNEY: "What lies do you tell your girlfriends?"

WEEKS: "I'm not cheating on them."

Five years, Carney told Weeks. Five years, five murders. Carney was in high dudgeon now. His client, Whitey, was paying close attention.

CARNEY: "You played the system like a pro, Mr. Weeks, didn't you?"

Objection. Sustained.

CARNEY: "You knew how the system would work, didn't you, Mr. Weeks, didn't you?. . . You won against the system?"

WEEKS: "What did I win? What did I win?"

CARNEY: "You won five years."

WEEKS: "Five people are dead! Five people are dead!"

CARNEY: "Does that bother you at all?"

WEEKS: "Yeah, it bothers me."

CARNEY: "How does it bother you?"

WEEKS: "Because we killed people that were rats, and I had the two biggest rats right next to me. That's why it—"

Now, finally, after all these days, Whitey snapped. He looked up at his so-called surrogate son and hissed, "You suck."

Weeks immediately jumped up and glared at Whitey: "Fuck you, okay?"

By now the judge was also standing up as the exchange continued.

WHITEY: "Fuck you too!"

WEEKS: "What do you want to do?"

Then it was over, as quickly as it had begun. The judge, still standing, told "Mr. Bulger" to let his lawyers do his talking for him and she ordered "Mr. Weeks" to answer the questions. Then she sat back down and told Carney to continue.

CARNEY: "You don't really care about the five people, do you?"

Objection. Argumentative. Sustained.

CARNEY: "It doesn't matter to you that you killed those five people, does it?"

Same objection. Overruled.

WEEKS: "I didn't kill those people. Your client killed those people, not me."

CARNEY: "You pleaded guilty to it, didn't you?"

WEEKS: "Aiding and abetting."

CARNEY: "And that's the same thing as you pulling the trigger, isn't it?"

WEEKS: "I was there. We're all guilty."

CARNEY: "And your guilt doesn't bother you in the slightest, does it?"

WEEKS: "You don't know what bothers me."

CARNEY: "Nothing bothers you, except you?"

WEEKS: "No, that's not true."

CARNEY: "I have nothing further."

WEEKS: "I keep things to myself."

JUDGE CASPER: "Mr. Weeks, the questions are finished."

4

Ruse

In one of his many court appearances, Kevin Weeks was asked how Whitey's gang could get away with all that they did in America.

"We weren't in America," Weeks said. "We were in Boston."

And in Boston, his boss Whitey controlled the cops, to a greater or lesser degree, depending on the department. But Whitey had people everywhere, which meant that even a non-criminal—a civilian, you might say—had to worry about having Whitey find out that he was talking to the cops.

Dickie O'Brien in wheelchair

That's what he told Michael Solimando, but most of the gang's victims already knew that they couldn't even consider going to the police. In fact, in the early days of the investigation that finally brought him down, most of them willingly

Angiulo brothers at the grand jury; Jerry is second from right

took an 18-month sentence for contempt of court rather than testify against the criminals who had threatened to kill them.

The extortions started with the bookies. In the beginning, when Winter Hill first came together in the early 1970's, they planned to actually run a gambling operation, like Bernie McGarry or Doc Sagansky or the Angiulos, handling layoffs for bookies. It was Whitey's idea to get into sports betting, though. Jerry Angiulo warned them about sports. The odds on the numbers were a steady 600 to one, day in and day out. But sports—a local team could get hot, and if you didn't know what you were doing, if you didn't make enough layoffs, you could get burnt. Badly.

"Bring a barrel of money," Angiulo warned them. They didn't have a barrel of money, so they had to borrow one, from Angiulo. That was something they never quite figured out about Jerry—he didn't care so much about the numbers or any of his other gambling enterprises as he did about the money he could lend when his customers got into trouble. The numbers—and the high-stakes card games, and the barbooth games—were all tools to produce the real customers, the shylocking victims.

In the early 1970's, the Mass. State Lottery had been started, and although at first it was only one, and then two, nights a week, the trend was obvious. The state was muscling into the numbers racket, and they wouldn't tolerate any competition.

The State Lottery was run by the elected treasurer, Bob Crane, a former legislative colleague of Whitey's brother. By the early 1980's, at his St. Patrick's Day breakfast every year, Senate president Bulger would introduce Crane as "the biggest bookie in the state."

He wasn't kidding.

By the time the original Winter Hill Gang broke up, Whitey and Stevie were left owing $250,000 to Angiulo. They promised they'd pay $5,000 but never did. They did keep up the "vig"—$2,500 a week—for awhile, but eventually stopped paying anything.

Jerry Angiulo was not happy, as he made clear on the FBI tapes from 98 Prince Street that were now being transcribed.

"Jesus Christ all fuckin' mighty, why haven't these guys been in touch with me? I don't understand it. Fuck me maybe, they don't like me. They got a right not to like me. That's their right . . . But they been jerkin' me around."

And why not? They knew, even if Jerry didn't, that he wasn't going to be around once the FBI finished transcribing those tapes. And so Whitey got out from under what he owed.

But he and Stevie had learned their lesson. They now had zero interest in the numbers, or anything else that resembled a game of "chance." They wanted no chances, just "rent."

In other words, shakedowns.

Dick O'Brien, an 84-year-old retired bookie from Quincy, was asked on the witness stand to describe the difference between working for the Angiulos as opposed to Whitey and Stevie.

"I thought it was like night and day. The Angiulos were very, very businesslike. This was no rent being paid. You gave them your business, layoffs, and they took the opportunity to win or lose. And when it was Stevie and Mr. Bulger, they weren't interested in that. They were interested in the rent."

O'Brien was an old friend of Johnny Martorano's, so Whitey did offer him a few extra services not available to all of their "tenants." One time O'Brien had a bookie from Brockton named George Labate who had run up a number of debts—"makeups"—and then gone missing.

Finally Labate turned up and O'Brien took him to the Tara Hotel in Braintree for a little chat with Whitey.

"Mr. Bulger said to him, 'Were you treated right by Dick?' And Labate says yes I was. He said, 'What are you doing? You owe him a big amount in makeup but you stopped calling him.'"

Labate tried giving Whitey the old song-and-dance about how sure, he'd pay Dick back what he owed him, but that he wanted to get into his own business.

Whitey smiled. He told Labate that he had a second business too. What's that? Labate asked.

"Killing assholes like you," he said. When O'Brien told the story from the witness stand, Whitey chuckled. It was so unusual that Wyshak would mention it in his closing.

Another time, O'Brien was having problems with a bookie named Jim Timilty. He was brought to the gang's garage on Lancaster Street for his come-to-Jesus moment. Whitey and Stevie took Timilty into an office while O'Brien waited outside. Timilty finally emerged, and he and O'Brien left in Dick's car. O'Brien asked him where he wanted to be dropped off.

"Someplace I can get a drink," he said.

The older bookies were more afraid of Stevie than Whitey. They remembered him in his pre-lam days, when he was wiping out the McLaughlins and then the Bennetts. O'Brien, like at least one other extortion victim, preferred to stop by Triple O's and leave his monthly "rent" with Kevin O'Neil.

"When I could I'd rather pay Mr. O'Neil than to listen to anything that Mr. Flemmi might have had to say, because he wasn't always a happy person."

In the end, O'Brien went to prison rather than testify against the gang. He was in Plymouth with everybody else—Stevie, the Martoranos, Frank Salemme—and they told him, don't worry about it, next time you're called to testify, put everything on George Kaufman.

George Kaufman

George Kaufman was one of the gang, and he'd been indicted too. The difference was, he was dying of cancer. It was a Hill tradition, putting it on the dead guy—just like Whitey and his "immunity deal" from the late Jeremiah O'Sullivan.

Another bookie who went to the can was James Katz, now 72. He was incarcerated for lying to the grand jury in July 1993.

"If I were to testify, I felt my safety would—it would have been compromised, probably . . . You could wind up in a hospital, let's put it that way."

Katz was one of the first witnesses at the trial, and as he kept referring to "the Bulger Group," Jay Carney protested that the description was prejudicial to his client. A sidebar conference was called and Katz listened as the judge told him to stop using the phrase "Bulger Group."

"How about 'the Mob'?" Katz suggested.

THIS WAS before the more gruesome extortions were recounted. Katz served only a few months in prison before he was released, after he decided to become a cooperating witness and "cleanse" himself of his perjury.

In his cross-examination, Carney seemed to take Katz' travails lightly.

CARNEY: "Was there anyone in the prison to, like, gently touch you?"

KATZ: "You mean to befriend me, is that what you're saying?"

CARNEY: "I'm talking about the kind of touch on your arm that your wife might make, gently and loving?"

KATZ: "I don't know where you're going to, but nobody like my wife was in prison that I met."

WILLIAM DAVID Lindholm didn't get a funny cross-examination with Woody Allen-esque questions. Age 62, Lindholm was a bigtime marijuana dealer in the 1980's. He used to bet with Joe Yerardi, who was handling Johnny Martorano's money for him while he was on the lam in Florida.

On Independence Day, 1983, Lindholm was on Nantucket with his wife. He bumped into Joey Y, who was with Jimmy Martorano and his young son. They socialized, and a few days later, back in Boston, Yerardi and Martorano asked him to meet them at the Aquarium. They might have an opportunity for him, they said.

Lindholm ended up at the Marconi Club in Roxbury, Stevie's headquarters.

Yerardi and Martorano brought him upstairs to what passed for a banquet room, but Lindholm "wasn't feeling comfortable about the situation." Especially when his hosts disappeared. He saw four men in the function hall, and two of them frisked him. The other two guys were Whitey Bulger and Stevie Flemmi. Whitey asked him if he knew why he was

Joey Yerardi

there. Lindholm mentioned that business opportunity he'd been told about. Whitey shook his head.

"He paused and he looked at me. And there was a cart with some towels on top of the cart, and he and another individual pulled out two guns from underneath the towels and they said, 'No, that's not why you're here. You're here because you're not with somebody.'"

Then Whitey began yelling. Eventually he demanded a million dollars. Lindholm, a veteran of tense negotiations with South American drug dealers, hung tough. But Whitey could play tougher.

"One of the persons fired off a gun by my head, and there was a silencer on it, and the chamber was opened, and five bullets were knocked on the table with one spent casing. And a bullet was put in the chamber and spun and pointed at my head, and the trigger was pulled."

Like Russian roulette, he was asked?

"Right."

Eventually, he got Bulger down to $250,000. Lindholm was still mystified; he did no business in Southie, and he'd never told Yerardi about his line of work. So it was just a speculative "ruse." As Lindholm left, with instructions on how to deliver the money, Bulger "shook my hand, told me that I handled myself well and some other people didn't handle themselves so well."

Prosecutor Zach Hafer: "Did Mr. Bulger say anything to you at the meeting, Mr. Lindholm, about what would happen if he found out you sold marijuana on your own without informing him?"

"Yes," said Lindholm. "He'd cut my head off."

WORD TRAVELS fast when people start to disappear. Threaten a few reporters, and the stories in the newspapers dry up. Kill a couple of businessmen, and they don't put up much of a fight when Whitey concocts another "ruse," a "crime of opportunity," as Kevin Weeks called it.

Michael Solimando's prep-school roommate had become an FBI agent. After his first visit to Triple O's, he thought about calling up his G-man friend. But then he sat down with his brother-in-law, Gene Kelly. He was another of the three people whose names Whitey threatened to put in a hat and then pick one out to kill if he didn't get the $400,000 he was "owed" for his alleged investment in the renovation of the building at 126 High Street. They kicked it around, whether or not to call the FBI agent.

"We talked and talked," Solimando testified, "and finally he (his brother-in-law) rationalized, 'We can't. There's just too many people dead in Boston for working with the authorities. There's too many bodies around. We've got to take this seriously.'"

Earlier, at Triple O's, Whitey had made the same point to Solimando, more colorfully.

"When he talked about going to law enforcement, he said other people thought they were going. He said, 'As a matter of fact, when we killed Halloran, they didn't know whether he died of lead poisoning or he was electrocuted, he had so many wires on him.' And him and Flemmi, they all laughed. They thought it was a big joke."

On his second trip to Triple O's, Solimando brought $20,000 cash. He also had with him a number of documents from the partnership with Callahan to prove that Whitey's murder victim hadn't invested anything close to $400,000 in 126 High Street.

Solimando was next summoned to the Lancaster Street garage. Stevie frisked him, and then Whitey told him to get in the backseat of a car, saying "Nobody can hear us in here. There's no bugs."

Obviously, the meeting took place after they had gotten the tip from their man in the State Police, Richard Schneiderhan, that the garage had been bugged. Solimando had another $20,000 cash, which he gave Whitey. Then Solimando asked him if he'd read the 126 High Street documents he'd brought to Triple O's earlier.

"And Mr. Flemmi said, 'We don't give a shit about the papers. That's all legal mumbo jumbo to us. We just want our money. He owes us the money. Get us the money.'"

The third partner, the lawyer, went to Switzerland and somehow removed $215,000 cash from a safe-deposit box Callahan had rented. That left close to $200,000 that Solimando and his brother-in-law had to raise from their businesses.

State Trooper Richard Schneiderhan

"We sold, you know, jewelry. We sold the cars. You know, we make money. You go out and—we had a restaurant. We had a construction company. We worked, and somehow we got it all together. We had stocks that I sold, anything we could do to liquidate. It took us time, but we did it."

> **HAFER:** "And you chose to pay them that instead of going to law enforcement?"
>
> **SOLIMANDO:** "It was either that or get killed."

RICHARD BUCCHERI knew both Whitey and Stevie. Now 73, he'd grown up with the Martoranos. He was in construction, a real-estate developer in Quincy. Stevie hired him to build the "shell" of the cabana—the sun porch—behind his mother's house in South Boston. Stevie finished the inside.

While his crews were there in Southie, he also did some repairs to the next-door house of Whitey's brother, Senate president William M. Bulger. His crews worked on the front entrance to the powerful politician's home, and to the stairs that led to the upstairs.

PROSECUTOR KELLY: "Who paid you to do that?"

BUCCHERI: "Mr. Flemmi."

Buccheri recounted basically the same story Weeks had told earlier in the trial. He had given a friend of his named Jack DePalma some advice in a dispute over a fence on some land Kevin Weeks was buying.

It didn't seem like a big deal, until Flemmi called. He said Jim Bulger wanted to see Buccheri in South Boston. With some trepidation, Buccheri finally agreed to have Stevie pick him up. But before he left Quincy, he called his daughter.

"I said I was going to South Boston and, God forbid, if something happens, you know. . . ."

Stevie drove him to the Bulger-Flemmi compound, and they got out and walked back to the sun porch. Whitey was sitting at a round table, and Buccheri and Flemmi sat down too.

"Mr. Bulger says to me, he says, 'You know, Rich, sometimes you could keep your mouth shut.' I says, 'What are you talking about?' He says, 'You said something about DePalma,' a fence and so forth, and he bangs the table."

To illustrate, Buccheri slammed his hand down on the witness stand.

"He says, 'Do you know that Kevin Weeks is my surrogate son?' I says, 'I don't even know who Kevin Weeks is, I never met him.'"

Wrong answer.

"With that, he takes the shotgun that was on the table, sticks it in my mouth. I went back, Stevie moved back. I looked at him. Mr. Bulger took the shotgun out, and he hits me in the shoulder and says, 'Rich, you know, you're a standup guy, I'm not going to kill you.'"

KELLY: "Did he make threats about your family?"

BUCCHERI: "Yes. He says, 'I'm not going to kill you now, all right?' but he says, 'It's going to cost you.' 'Cost me what?' He says, '200.' I said, 'What, $200?' He says, 'No, $200,000.' With that, he puts his hand on the chair next to him, takes a .45, puts it to my head, and he says, 'If you don't pay me in 30 days I'm going to kill you and your family.' I says, 'Okay.' He puts the gun down."

Then he told Stevie to make the arrangements on how to get the money. Stevie and Buccheri left and drove back to Quincy. On the way south, Flemmi told him, "Don't worry about it."

"I says, 'I don't have $200,000 in cash.' I says, 'Will you take a check?' He said, 'Yeah, give me a check.'"

Buccheri got the money together and made the check out so that it appeared to be a real-estate deal. This was on a Friday. On Monday Flemmi cashed the $200,000 check, after which he telephoned Buccheri.

"He said that Jim said you're a friend now."

KELLY: "Who said you were a friend?"

BUCCHERI: "Jim Bulger said I was a friend."

KELLY: "Did you ever talk to Bulger again?"

BUCCHERI: "No sir."

In his closing, Fred Wyshak mentioned this particular "ruse."

"You know the old saying," he said. "With friends like this, who needs enemies?"

Jackie Bulger, Bureau of Prisons #23989-038, leaving courthouse

"Up to Our Necks in Murders"

It was June 17, 2013—Bunker Hill Day, a local "hack holiday" for all the members of the Bulger family who were on public payrolls, which at one time was almost all of them, including Whitey himself.

At one St. Patrick's Day breakfast in the late 1980's, then-Senate president Billy Bulger had pointed out one of his sisters to then-Gov. Michael S. Dukakis.

"This is my sister Carol McCarthy," Whitey's brother had said in the packed room known locally as Halitosis Hall. "Would you believe it, she's not on a public payroll."

"I don't believe it," said the governor. Indeed, a few months later she too was on a state payroll, enjoying Bunker Hill Day as a paid holiday.

John Martorano

But the federal courts are always open on Bunker Hill Day. It was Day 4 in the trial of former Suffolk County courthouse janitor James J. Bulger, Jr.

"Your Honor," said prosecutor Fred Wyshak, "the government's next witness is John Martorano."

"He may be called," said Judge Denise J. Casper.

Martorano, at age 72, still looked like a Hollywood hitman from Central Casting—built like the All-State fullback he once was, hair combed straight back, his answers laconic, just as he had been taught by his federal handlers.

He'd been through this routine at least twice before—at the racketeering trial of corrupt FBI agent Zip Connolly in Boston in 2004, and then at Zip's murder trial in Miami in 2008. In Florida, Connolly's lawyer said he felt intimidated by Martorano, but the jury believed him. Connolly was now doing 40 years for second-degree murder.

The only question for "the Cook," as Whitey and Stevie called their partner, was how hard this team of defense lawyers would come after him. Hank Brennan gave him his answer the instant he began his cross-examination the next day.

"Mr. Martorano," he began, without introducing himself, "you are a mass murderer, are you not?"

"I don't think so."

"You've killed for friends, right?"

"Correct."

"You've killed for family?"

"Correct."

"You've killed young, haven't you?"

"It was an accident."

"Have you killed young, Mr. Martorano?"

"Yes."

"You've killed people that you've known, true?"

"Correct."

"You've killed friends? Yes?"

"Correct."

"You've killed strangers?"

"Correct."

Disgraced ex-FBI agent John "Zip" Connolly on his way to his racketeering trial

"You've killed innocent people, haven't you?"

"Correct."

"You don't like the term 'hitman,' do you, Mr. Martorano?"

"Not especially."

"Mr. Callahan gave you $50,000 after you killed Mr. Wheeler for him, didn't he?"

"Correct."

It didn't seem terribly effective in undercutting Martorano as a witness, but it was all Brennan could do. Like the earlier defense attorneys, Brennan wasn't going to have much success shaking Martorano's story. A day earlier Wyshak had gone over the names that were already becoming familiar to the members of the jury.

Six times Martorano had answered "yes" when Wyshak asked him if he had pleaded guilty to the murders of, in order, Michael Milano, Al Plummer, William O'Brien, James O'Toole, Roger Wheeler and John Callahan.

Six other times he had answered "correct" when Wyshak asked him if he had pleaded guilty to the murders of, in order, Joe Notarangeli, Al Notarangeli, James Sousa, Thomas King, Edward Connors and Richard Castucci.

Twelve murders, 14 years, of which he served 12½ years. Not enough, the prosecutors would say time and again. Not nearly enough. And that wasn't even a complete list of his victims—he'd admitted committing eight other murders he was never charged with. Between the ages of 24 and 41 he murdered 20 men and women, 15 whites and five blacks, in three states. He killed them in garages, in phone booths, at stop signs, and in coffee shops. He'd killed them drunk and he'd killed them high, and dumped them in alleys, ditches and in the trunks of their own cars.

But without his testimony . . . there would be no case.

"Can you tell us," said Wyshak, "what your relationship was with James Bulger and Stephen Flemmi?"

"They were my partners in crime. They were my best friends. They were my children's godfathers."

"And what motivated you to cooperate against them?"

"Well, after I heard that they were informants, it sort of broke my heart. But, you know, they broke all trust that we had, all loyalties, and I was just beside myself with it."

Beyond the murders, the prosecutors had another problem to explain to the jury. After lengthy negotiations, which included months "in the hole" for Martorano at the federal prison at Otisville, NY, the feds had agreed that he would only have to testify against Whitey and Stevie, as well as corrupt cops.

The names of a few gangsters from South Boston had been added to the plea agreement, but they were mere window dressing. Martorano barely even knew those guys from across the Broadway bridge. The gangsters he knew—that he'd murdered people with—he didn't have to testify against them. Howie Winter, the other original leader of the Winter Hill Gang. Pat Nee, the affable Irish-born Vietnam vet and leader of the Mullens gang in Southie. And even more importantly, his younger brother Jimmy Martorano. Johnny had confessed to the crimes that they'd committed with the three of them, including murders. He just didn't have to go on the witness stand and point the finger at them. It would have been against his code. As for the others, Stevie and Whitey—"you can't rat a rat," he always said. For months he'd talked to the cops in three states. He'd cleared up dozens of previously unsolved murders dating back to the 1960's.

Surveillance photo of Stevie and Whitey

"During the course of that de-briefing, did you confess to the murders of eight other individuals that you committed during the 1960's?"

"Yes."

One by one, Wyshak asked him if he killed Robert Palladino, John Jackson, Anthony Veranis, Ronald Hicks, Herbert Smith, Douglas Barrett and Elizabeth Dickson.

Yes, he said. Yes, yes, yes, yes, yes, yes, yes.

"And you've never been charged with those murders, is that fair to say?"

"Never."

Howie Winter

He was released from prison in 2007. Since then, he had sold the rights to his life story to Graham King, the producer of *The Departed*, the movie widely regarded as based on the life of Whitey Bulger, although the original script was written for a Chinese film. He'd received an initial payment of $250,000, with more to come if it's ever filmed.

He also agreed to a book deal with the author of this book. The advance was $110,000, and the royalties so far have amounted to another $70,000 or so, all of which has been split equally between the writer and Martorano. The book was on *The New York Times* bestseller list for four weeks in 2011. The title of the book: *Hitman*. It was another detail that prosecutor Wyshak had to get on the record.

"Mr. Martorano, were you a hitman?"

"No."

Pat Nee

"Did anybody ever pay you to kill people?"

"No."

"Why did you let Mr. Carr name the book *Hitman*?"

"He thought it would sell better."

From an early age, Martorano moved easily among the various underworld factions in Boston. His father owned Luigi's, an after-hours joint in the city's red-light district, the Combat Zone, that was frequented by hoodlums from all the various crews. He wasn't associated with one particular neighborhood; he grew up in suburban Milton. He was half-Irish, half-Italian. He had an easy way about him, and was friendly with hookers, cops, burglars, bookies and killers.

Jimmy Martorano

In 1964, a waitress at his father's club was murdered. His brother Jimmy was a suspect. Stevie Flemmi told him that two guys who had been at Luigi's that night, Robert Palladino and John Jackson, were going to testify against Jimmy.

In November 1965, Jimmy and Johnny picked up Palladino at an after-hours joint on Blue Hill Avenue.

"He got a shot off, and then I shot him."

Martorano was 24 years old. He and Jimmy dumped the body at the North Station. With several of Joe Barboza's gang, Johnny shotgunned John Jackson to death a year or so later.

Robert Palladino

One of Johnny's best friends and drinking buddies was a Dorchester gunsel named Billy O'Sullivan. O'Sullivan opened an after-hours joint in Roxbury, and Johnny brought a date to the grand opening. But he ran into an ex-con boxer from Southie who had beaten up Jimmy Martorano the night before in Southie while Jimmy was trying to collect some money Veranis owed him.

"He started mouthing off about how he just gave my brother a beating, some stuff like that, and 'F' him, 'F' you, and went to pull a gun, and I shot him."

John Jackson

It was the end of Billy O's new club. Johnny owed him, and it was Whitey Bulger who would call in the chit a few years later.

By then, though, Johnny had killed five more people. Three blacks he shot to death during a snowstorm in Roxbury; he was trying to avenge a beating of Stevie Flemmi when he killed a 19-year-old girl and a 17-year-old boy, in addition to the middle-aged bouncer he'd meant to shoot.

"I felt terrible," he told Wyshak. "But you can't change it."

A few months later, he shot to death a black coke dealer named Ronald Hicks, who was going to testify in a triple-homicide case against two black brothers named Campbell. Martorano didn't know them, but he did know

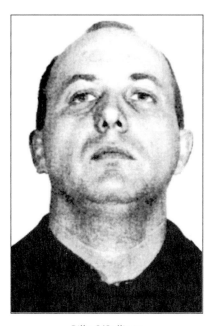

Billy O'Sullivan

one of their wives. She asked him for help. Wyshak asked Martorano how he decided to help.

"I shot Hicks," he said.

A year later, in 1969, he stabbed a pimp to death outside the Sugar Shack. He was out on a date at the time. His date drove the car while he was killing the pimp, whose name was "Touch."

In 1972, Martorano had a small bar on Columbus Ave. in the South End. He and his brother and Howie Winter were doing renovations on a new, larger club down at the corner of Columbus and Dartmouth. It was to be called Chandler's, and in the meantime they were using their new liquor license on a little dive down the street, Duffy's. It had become Johnny's hangout. After hours, with the lights out, he would sit by himself and shoot rats as they came out of the walls. There were a lot of rats at Duffy's.

One night another one walked into Duffy's, on two feet.

"Whitey introduced himself, and said he was a friend of a friend of mine, Billy O'Sullivan. And Billy O'Sullivan just got killed in the Southie gang war."

So now he was calling in the favor Johnny owed Billy. Whitey, like O'Sullivan, was working for longtime Southie rackets czar Donald Killeen, who was losing a gang war to the Mullens, a younger crew that

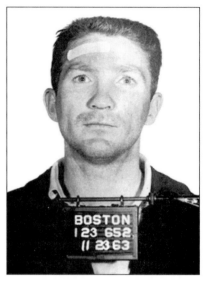

Tony Veranis

Ronald Hicks, potential witness against the Campbells and Chandler, murdered by Johnny Martorano in 1968

Whitey with parrot—was its name Zip?

included several Vietnam combat veterans. Now Whitey was asking Johnny to get his pal Howie Winter to intervene with the Mullens to end the war.

An armistice was arranged. The only hang-up was what would happen to Donald Killeen. It was decided he would have to go. He went, shot to death in this car in Framingham in May 1972, after his 4-year-old son's birthday party. Whitey would always claim he had nothing to do with it. Killeen's Lower End bar, the Transit Café, quickly ended up in the hands of one of Whitey's underlings, Kevin O'Neil, and two of his brothers. Its new name: Triple O's.

Donald Killeen

Jerry Angiulo

Next Whitey suggested a merger among the Southie gangs and the Somerville crews run by Howie Winter, Joe McDonald and Jimmy Sims. Whitey said there was plenty of money to be made, "rounding up" any independent bookmakers that the Mafia didn't get to first.

"In Town," the local Mafia run by Jerry Angiulo, went along with this new arrangement.

> **WYSHAK:** "What kind of relationship did you have with Mr. Angiulo?
>
> **MARTORANO:** "I don't know how to put that. We knew each other."

Now that he had some "partners" who had just been through a long and bloody gang war, Angiulo decided to call in his own chit. One of his bookies, Paulie Folino, had just been murdered

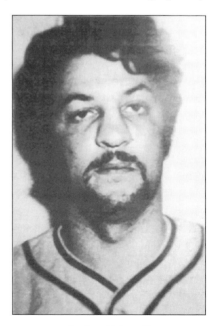

Indian Al Angeli

by a hotheaded bookie named Al Notarangeli, or, as he called himself, Angeli. Indian Al.

Indian Al was doing a bit up in Vermont for torching an inn he owned, and he'd lost all of his bookmaking customers except one, a guy named Joe Mann. He turned Mann over to his brother, Indian Joe, and his partner, Charlie Raso.

"That was his only means of income at the time," Raso would testify.

So when Paulie Folino took Joe Mann away from Indian Al, he went crazy. On his next weekend furlough from prison, he found Folino, hogtied him and threw him into a shallow grave on a golf course. As Folino's muscles relaxed, the rope tightened and slowly strangled him. "He died hard," a cop said later.

Now Angiulo called in his new partners, Howie Winter and Johnny Martorano and filled them in on Indian Al.

"He said he was a loose cannon, that he was very dangerous, and we should be watching out for him ourselves."

John Hurley

Angiulo asked the Hill to take him out. They agreed. They posted lookouts at Raso's bar in North Station, Mother's, where Indian Al was hanging out now that he'd been released from prison. On the night of March 8, 1973, a Charlestown hood named John Hurley radioed that Indian Al was in the bar. Two cars left from Marshall Street on Winter Hill and arrived shortly after last call. It was 2:00 in the morning.

The first "boiler," as the gang called the stolen cars they used on hits, was driven by the Hill's top wheelman, Jimmy Sims. Armed with machine guns were Howie Winter and Johnny Martorano, the first team. The "crash car," which would be used to run into any pursuing police vehicles, had to be legitimate. This night they were using a car belonging to one of Whitey's Southie hoods, Jack Curran. Whitey, the second-best driver in the gang, was behind the wheel.

Both cars followed the brown Mercedes—Indian Al's car, apparently. As the three cars approached Brighton Center, the Mercedes came to a halt at a stop sign.

"We pulled up to the side and gave it what you'd call a 'broadside'—both guns shooting at it."

WYSHAK: "Now, was Al Notarangeli in the car that night?"

MARTORANO: "No, he wasn't."

WYSHAK: "Who did you learn was in that car?"

MARTORANO: "A guy named Michael Milano."

WYSHAK: "And did Milano die?"

MARTORANO: "Yes, he did."

WYSHAK: "He was the wrong guy. Is that fair to say?"

MARTORANO: "Wrong guy."

Whitey, however, was quite impressed by the fireworks.

"He said it looked like the car exploded."

Ten days later, they again thought they had Indian Al, this time on Commercial Street on the North End. Same first team: Sims driving, Winter and Martorano shooting, Whitey in the crash car. Sims had to cut in front of the Notarangeli car, with Winter and Martorano firing through the boiler's back window. One of Indian Al's crew was killed—a guy named Al "Bud" Plummer—but the others escaped. Driving behind, Whitey almost didn't.

"He thought he was going to get shot, because there's

Plummer's car at the crime scene

tracer bullets in the machine gun, and they were going over his head when he was behind us."

Wyshak asked, "Was he angry?"

"Well," said Martorano, "sort of joking about it."

Next they killed a guy on Morrissey Boulevard named William O'Brien. It was Dorchester, Whitey's territory, so he was driving. The passenger, an ex-con named Ralph DeMasi, survived, and would be testifying himself in a few days.

Then Jimmy Sims and Joe McDonald drove to Fort Lauderdale and murdered a fugitive member of Indian Al's gang named James Leary. McDonald chased him around a trailer before shooting him five times in the

William O'Brien

face. The feds had a photo of Leary to show the jury, but the bodies were piling up so fast now that they didn't even bother to put it up on the screen. After all, Whitey hadn't been charged with that murder.

By this time, Indian Al's brother Indian Joe had had enough. He hadn't killed Paulie Folino, he wanted a truce. Figuring In Town was doing the killing, he called Howie Winter for the same reason Whitey Bulger had reached out to him a year earlier—to broker a deal.

Howie was given a number where he could reach Indian Joe at a certain time. Johnny Martorano figured he could find out where the phone booth was. He called the phone company and got a superintendent on the line.

Indian Joe, before he took the phone call at the Pewter Pot

"I told him my kid was at that phone booth, and he was looking—waiting for me to pick him up, but he ran out of change before he told me the address, and I don't know where it is. So the superintendent got on and gave me the address."

It was the Pewter Pot restaurant in Medford Square. Once again, John Hurley was given the assignment of identifying one of the Notarangelis.

MARTORANO: "I told him, don't make a mistake again."

WYSHAK: "What did he say to you?"

MARTORANO: "He came out and said, 'That's him.'"

WYSHAK: "What did you do?"

MARTORANO: "I went in and shot him."

WYSHAK: "Where did you shoot him?

MARTORANO: "In the heart."

Indian Al ran away, and didn't return until March 1974. Then, like his late brother Joe, Indian Al called Howie Winter and asked him to set up a meeting with Jerry Angiulo. Johnny and Howie took Indian Al to the Café Pompeii in the North End, where he sat down with Angiulo, as Winters and Martorano took a table a few feet away. Indian Al admitted murdering Paulie Folino, and then handed Angiulo a bag containing $50,000 for Folino's family.

Angiulo told Indian Al that from now on, if he wanted to do anything, he'd

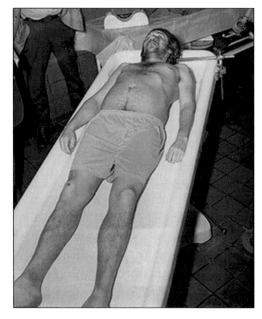

Indian Joe at the morgue

have to do it with Howie. Then Howie and Johnny drove him away, after which they returned to the Pompeii and split up the $50,000 with Angiulo. "Expenses," it was called. Then Jerry told them to kill Indian Al.

A week or so later, Angiulo called the Hill.

"He was wondering what was taking so long."

"What does that mean," Wyshak asked, " 'what's taking so long?' "

"Why isn't Al dead?"

Eventually, Indian Al called. Howie and Johnny drove to Revere to meet them. Johnny was in the backseat. He shot Indian Al in the head. Whitey was in the crash car.

In December 1973, they killed Spike O'Toole, one of the last remaining McLaughlin gang members. They caught up with him as he walked out of a barroom on Savin Hill Ave in Dorchester.

Again, in Dorchester Whitey was the driver. As he left the bar, O'Toole saw the guns pointing at him from the boiler. He tried to hide behind a mailbox, which he kept moving around in front of him. As Martorano was shooting at O'Toole, some civilians began walking

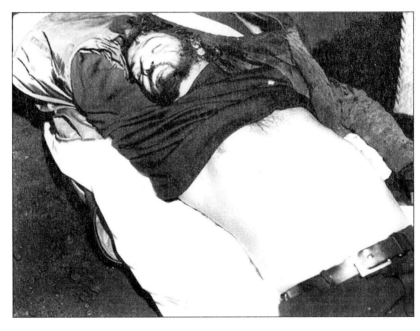

Indian Al at the morgue

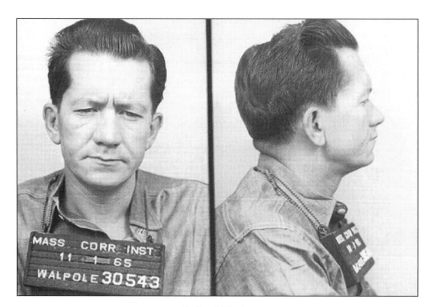

Spike O'Toole

across the avenue. Whitey had to wave them off—with his hand. After they had finished off O'Toole and returned to Somerville, he told the others he'd learned a lesson.

"He said, you know, I'm never going to be in a car without a gun again."

Soon the Hill was involved in fixing horse races up and down the East Coast. Tony Ciulla, a local swindler, was running the grift, along with a strong-arm named Billy Barnoski. Angiulo told the Hill that Ciulla was no damn good, but by then they were making too much money to quit.

But Ciulla had other scams going. One involved fake gold bars, and for the ripoff of a dentist, Ciulla recruited a drunk who'd been staying at Barnoski's apartment, James Sousa. Joe McDonald, one of the Hill partners, also was going to take part.

The "exchange" was supposed to take place in the supermarket parking lot across Broadway from the gang's garage. But the dentist showed up with his kid, and a firearm, and gunfire broke out when the dentist realized the "gold" was in fact bricks. Sousa was arrested, and he was frantic. Ciulla came over to the garage to lobby for the gang to clip Sousa.

The six partners—Stevie Flemmi had returned from the lam by this point—met to decide what to do.

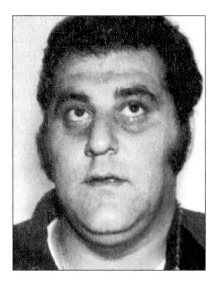

Tony Ciulla

Billy Barnoski

"We decided to kill Sousa. I wanted to kill Ciulla, but they said no," testified Martorano.

They told Sousa to come over to the garage and they'd give him some money for a lawyer. He left his laundry at his estranged wife's house on the South Shore and then drove to the garage. Johnny shot him in the head. He was buried in a state park in Boxford; his body has never been found.

(Barnoski died in September 2013 in Leominster, at the age of 74, while serving a life sentence for the murder of Lowell bookie Jackie McDermott in 1988.)

Wyshak ran him through more murders—Richie Castucci, set up by Zip Connolly. Tom King, set up by Whitey, after which he went to "Plan B," as Martorano called it, killing another of his old Mullen foes, Buddy Leonard, and then leaving the body in King's car.

WYSHAK: "Was Winter Hill a democracy, so to speak?"

MARTORANO: "So to speak."

He talked about how the race-fixing scheme went bad after Ciulla was arrested and flipped. Before he could be indicted, Martorano then went

Richie Castucci

on the lam with Patty Lytle. She was a Somerville High dropout from Ball Square whom he'd started dating when she was 15.

Next, the prosecutor took Martorano through the World Jai Alai murder spree. Under questioning, Martorano explained how his friend John Callahan, an Ivy League accountant by day, "wanted to hang out with the rogues at night." Callahan had once run a company called World Jai Alai and now wanted to buy it from its new owner, Roger

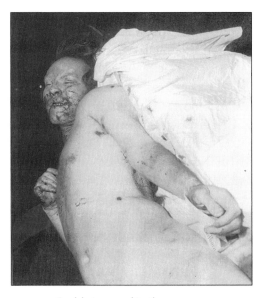

Buddy Leonard in the morgue

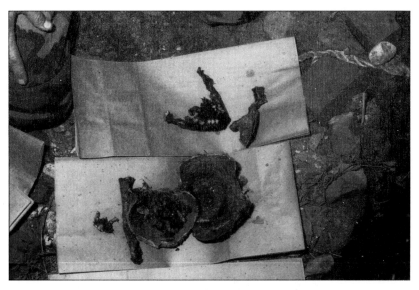

Tommy King's skull

Wheeler, a millionaire businessman who lived in Tulsa. The company's director of security was now-retired FBI agent H. Paul Rico, Stevie's old handler when he was an informant in the 1960's.

Everything would be so good if they could just get rid of Wheeler, Callahan told Martorano. He'd even cut the Hill in for $10,000 a week on the parking-lot skim; in return, they'd keep the Mafia out of the company's Connecticut fronton.

But first Wheeler had to go. He wouldn't sell and he was trying to get proof that Callahan had been skimming company profits. So Callahan made the pitch: would Martorano kill him? Martorano said he had to clear it with Whitey and Stevie. But then Callahan had another idea. He would use one of his drinking buddies, the Winter Hill hanger-on Brian Halloran. He broached the idea to Halloran at a meeting attended by Whitey and Stevie. Then Callahan thought better of it; he gave Halloran $20,000 in cash and told him to forget about it.

Instead, the task of eliminating Wheeler fell to Martorano. His driver would be fellow Winter Hill fugitive Joe McDonald, who was also living in Florida. Now it was H. Paul Rico calling in a chit—he'd allowed the late Winter Hill boss Buddy McLean to hide out in his house after a 1964 hit. So McDonald owed him one—one murder.

Martorano said he never really believed Rico was involved in the murder plot to kill Wheeler until he got a detailed description of Wheeler's routine in his hometown of Tulsa, including a description of Wheeler's "ruddy" complexion.

"I never read it before, 'ruddy,' except as an FBI description."

On May 27, 1981, Martorano caught up with Wheeler in the parking lot of a golf course in Tulsa. Joe McDonald was driving the "boiler"—the stolen getaway car.

But that wasn't the last of the World Jai Alai murders. In May 1982, Whitey took out Brian Halloran, who had started talking to the FBI after he was arrested for the murder of a drug dealer in Chinatown. After the Halloran murder, Martorano flew to New York to meet Stevie and Whitey at the LaGuardia Marriott in New York.

In a hotel room, Whitey told him he'd killed Halloran to save Martorano's life, neglecting to mention that Halloran was also pointing the finger at him and Stevie. Whitey told Martorano he now had to kill Callahan, because he wouldn't "stand up." Martorano didn't want to do it. He liked Callahan, he owed him, and it seemed crazy to kill "a guy I just killed a guy for."

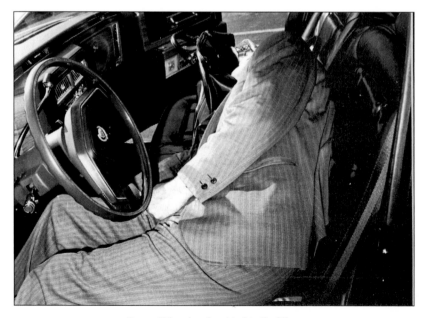

Roger Wheeler dead in his Cadillac

"I felt lousy, but you know, these were my partners, you know, it sort of dictated. We were up to our necks in murders already, this is—this is what they wanted. I have to do it. They just convinced me they just saved my life."

On July 31, 1982, Callahan flew to Fort Lauderdale for the weekend. Martorano picked him up at the airport and shot him to death in the airport parking garage. Joe McDonald again drove the backup car. The defense would have many more questions for Martorano about this murder.

Later, Martorano's two "partners" began to tire of supporting him. He'd been an invaluable asset when they had to worry about possible moves against their now-tiny gang by the Mafia. He was the Mafia's "bogeyman," as Zip Connolly put it. But now In Town had more problems with law enforcement than with what was left of Winter Hill. Plus, many of Johnny's old associates were getting up there in age, and often, like Dick O'Brien, were retiring to Florida themselves.

Eventually Johnny set up a younger thug from Newton named Joe Yerardi, Joey Y, to handle the money he still had out on the street. Joey Y was into sports and shylocking, and he wasn't very good at either. By 1995 he owed Martorano $350,000. Then he too went on the lam, to Florida.

"I tried to salvage it," Martorano recalled, "with some kid, Arthur Gianelli was his buddy."

Arthur Gianelli—the brother-in-law of Zip Connolly. Somehow, someway, all roads seemed to lead back to Whitey.

At the end, Wyshak posed one final question to "the Cook."

"Mr. Martorano do you regret your life of crime?"

"Who wouldn't?"

AS HE began his cross-examination, Bulger attorney Hank Brennan returned to the subject of whether Martorano considered himself a hitman. That line of questioning went nowhere, so Brennan quickly switched to a different phrase.

"Explain to the jury why you're not a serial murderer."

"Because I don't consider myself one, that's why."

"Well, what is a serial murderer to you?"

"A serial murderer kills for fun," Martorano said. "They like it. I don't like it. I never did like it."

John Callahan's Cadillac with his body in the trunk

Joe Yerardi at the Lancaster Street Garage

"The 20 murders you admitted to, you didn't like any of them, sir?"

"No, I didn't like doing any of it. I don't like risking my life either."

"Well," Brennan said, "put aside risking your life right now, let's talk about the joy of it all."

"I never had any joy. I never had any joy at all."

"Well," said Brennan, "you're bragging about it in your books."

"I'm not bragging about it."

Brennan returned to the 1981 murder of Roger Wheeler in Tulsa.

Arthur Gianelli

"Although you say to this jury you're not a hitman, you got $50,000 from Mr. Callahan for killing Mr. Wheeler, right?"

"No," said Martorano. "He gave me that money in appreciation for me risking my life for him so he wouldn't go to jail. There was no talk about money for murder ever."

"You've said before that there was always a good reason when you would kill somebody," Brennan said. "Is that true?"

"I used to think that, yes."

"Is there any killing, any murder that wasn't justified, sir?"

"Ask me specifically, will you?"

Martorano acknowledged that he felt bad about killing

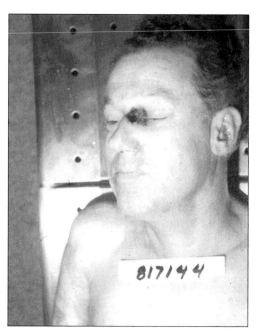

Roger Wheeler was killed with a single shot

the three blacks in the snowstorm. Also, Milano the lookalike bartender who he had thought was Indian Al.

"But I was told that by the other guy, it wasn't my mistake, it was somebody else's mistake."

"Well, that mistake caused an innocent person to be killed, didn't it?"

"Not my mistake."

"Who pulled the trigger?"

"I did."

"Who killed him?"

"I did."

In 2007, after his release from prison, Martorano had gone on *60 Minutes*. It was to be a favor to Ed Bradley, the CBS correspondent he briefly played football with at a Rhode Island prep school. Martorano's nickname was "the Milkman," because he always delivered. Bradley died shortly before Martorano's release from prison, but the Milkman delivered on his promise anyway. The substitute CBS reporter Steve Kroft asked many of the same types of questions Brennan was now throwing at Martorano, and Martorano eventually described himself as a "vigilante." Six years after Martorano first used the word, lawyer Brennan returned to the topic.

BRENNAN: "What did 'vigilante' mean to you?"

MARTORANO: "It's somebody that would hurt somebody that was doing wrong . . . like (Al) Notarangeli, he killed somebody."

BRENNAN: "And that makes you a vigilante like Batman, sir?"

MARTORANO: "I don't know about Batman."

Brennan asked him if Roger Wheeler had ever done anything to him that justified Martorano becoming a "vigilante" and shooting him in the head.

"No he didn't. In that case he was trying to put a friend of mine in jail."

BRENNAN: "And in your mind—"

MARTORANO: "In my mind, I helped my friend."

BRENNAN: "And as a vigilante, it was okay to murder him."

MARTORANO: "I would say in comparison to a serial killer."

Brennan went through most of Martorano's early murders in greater detail, then mentioned his statement on *60 Minutes* that he liked to be respected.

"Other than murdering all these people," Brennan asked, "what did you do to get respected, sir?"

"I always tried to help people, too."

"I see," Brennan said. "So the respect that everybody would have for you is because you murder people to help people."

"No, I always try to be a nice guy."

Which brought Brennan back to Martorano's murder of his good friend, Callahan. Martorano had stored Callahan's Cadillac in a rental storage garage before he picked him up and shot him. The plan was to leave Callahan's body in the trunk of his own car. After murdering him, Martorano and McDonald had to wait all night for the storage garage where they had left Callahan's Cadillac to open. Once the garage opened, at 7 a.m., they transferred Callahan's corpse from Johnny's minivan to his own Cadillac.

> BRENNAN: "When you put him in the trunk, you went for a cup of coffee after?"
>
> MARTORANO: "When he was in the car before the place opened, we went for a coffee to kill some time."

Kill some time. Unfortunate choice of words.

Whitey had wanted Martorano to bury Callahan. He told Flemmi and Weeks that there was "plenty of sand down there and he should have got off his fat ass" and dug a hole. Instead Martorano left Callahan's Cadillac at the Miami International Airport garage. Then he and McDonald took Callahan's personal effects and scattered them around Little Havana, to back up Zip Connolly's earlier 209's about the "bad Cubans" Callahan had taken up with.

Martorano later claimed Whitey never asked him to bury the body. As a matter of fact, Martorano had considered taking Callahan's body out in his new boat, chopping it up and then feeding it to the sharks. At any rate, even if Whitey had told Martorano to bury the body, it was ultimately Johnny's call. After all, Whitey and Johnny were partners, equals.

Garage in Miami where Callahan's personal effects were left

BRENNAN: "He wasn't your boss, was he?"

MARTORANO: "No, he was older than me, but he wasn't my boss."

BRENNAN: "Was he telling you what to do?"

MARTORANO: "Sometimes, yeah."

BRENNAN: "He would order you around, Mr. Martorano?"

MARTORANO: "Yeah, he would tell me sometimes what to do."

BRENNAN: "Really?"

MARTORANO: "If he wanted to get something done, I would usually listen to him. He usually knew the right buttons to press."

BRENNAN: "Was he your boss?"

MARTORANO: "No."

He wasn't, obviously. Because if Whitey had been his boss, somehow Whitey would have arranged it so that it would have been Martorano in the dock, and going back to solitary in Plymouth after court, while Whitey walked out of the courthouse door a free man. But now Martorano was the

John Martorano in his boat

free man, and Whitey was headed back to Plymouth in what had become known as the Ratmobile.

The Ratmobile leaving court

6

Garage Gallery

In January 1980, an informant of the Boston office of the FBI noted that what was left of the Winter Hill Gang had relocated its headquarters from the garage on Marshall Street in Somerville to Lancaster Street in the West End of Boston.

This intelligence was reported in the larger context of a murder. According to the informant, Whitey and Stevie had just killed a young bank robber in Charlestown—Stevie Hughes, Jr., the son of McLaughlin mobster Stevie Hughes, who had been shot to death in 1966 on Route 114 in Middleton.

The son was shot with a rifle as he got out of his car in the Charlestown housing projects. It was a "housekeeping" hit, eliminating someone who might someday think seriously about avenging his father's death.

The informant said the car used in the hit had been obtained from the recently opened Lancaster Foreign Car Service, operated by Winter Hill gangster George Kaufman.

The FBI, though, had no interest in following up on the information, either about the murder or about the gang's relocation. But that summer, when the State Police noticed a parade of gangland visitors going into the garage, they quickly set up a surveillance post in a building across the street and even planted a bug in a couch in the garage.

The bug was quickly compromised—the State Police blamed the FBI, but it appears the real culprit was one of the State Police's own, Richard

Schneiderhan, who accepted tens of thousands in payoffs over the years from first Johnny Martorano, then Stevie Flemmi and finally Kevin Weeks.

But the State Police did take a lot of surveillance photos before the gangsters relocated to a bank of phones at the old Howard Johnson's in Dorchester on the Southeast Expressway.

On Day 2 of the trial, June 13, 2013, many of the photos were introduced into evidence.

Lancaster Foreign Car Service

Whitey and Stevie enjoy a healthy snack—and some monkey business

Jackie Salemme, brother of Stevie's imprisoned former partner, Cadillac Frank Salemme

Whitey with Mafia capo Larry Baione, who once said, "We're the Hill and the
Hill is us, and we cannot tolerate them getting fucked"

Angelo Martorano, father of Johnny and Jimmy, shortly before his death

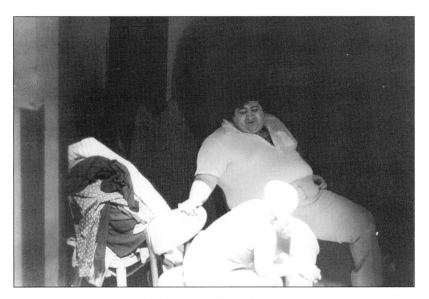

Bookmaker Fat Vinny Roberto

Up-and-coming Mafioso Vinnie "the Animal" Ferrara, a Boston College dropout

Stevie and Whitey with Nick Femia, former Barboza gang member. Femia was
shot to death in a botched robbery in East Boston in 1983

Frank Salemme, Jr. would eventually die of AIDS

Stevie Flemmi with Anthony D'Agostino, a/k/a "Tony Blue," former bodyguard
for Buddy McLean

Joe Mongiello, former cop and Winter Hill associate, with garage owner
George Kaufman

Richie O'Brien couldn't get away from Stevie Flemmi every day

Fidelity, Bravery, Integrity

It was June 27, 2013, the 12th day of the trial.

Prosecutor Fred Wyshak said, "Your Honor, the government's next witness is John Morris."

"He may be called," said Judge Casper.

Whitey Bulger didn't like a lot of the prosecution's witnesses, but he may have hated John Morris, the corrupt ex-FBI agent he paid $7,000 to in bribes over the years, more than anyone else.

After all, despite his outburst at Kevin Weeks, how much could he really complain? He did tell Weeks that if he got into a jam, "Put everything on me."

Morris, on the other hand, was supposed to be a cop. And he was the one Whitey blamed for the 1988 *Globe* series that he saw as the beginning of the end.

In fact, on the first day of Morris' testimony, once the jury was sent out of the courtroom for their mid-morning break, prosecutor Brian Kelly rose to address the judge.

Wyshak was handling Morris' direct examination, and Kelly was sitting at the prosecution table, a few feet away from Whitey. He could hear Whitey's muttering from the defense table.

"Counsel," said the judge, "before we break, Mr. Kelly, did you want to be heard on anything first?"

"I do your Honor," Kelly said. "Obviously Mr. Bulger has got a Sixth Amendment right to confront his accusers, but he doesn't have the right to sit at the defense table and say to the witness, 'You're a fuckin' liar' when the witness testifies, which is what he did earlier in Mr. Morris' testimony when Mr. Morris was talking about the Pallotta matter."

Earlier in the morning, Paulie McGonagle Jr. had testified about the murder of his father, and how Whitey had driven up to him a year later when he was 15. Whitey told him that they'd "taken care" of the guys who killed his father—namely, two of his father's best friends, whom Whitey himself had murdered the night before.

The brazen nature of Whitey's lies was still on everyone's mind in the courtroom as Kelly continued speaking about the defendant.

"Now, I know he spent his whole life trying to intimidate people, including 15-year-old boys in South Boston, but he should not be doing that here in federal court in the midst of trial. And I would respectfully ask the Court to admonish Mr. Bulger to keep his little remarks to himself when the witness is testifying."

Judge Casper said she hadn't heard the muttering, but she spoke directly to Bulger anyway.

"Just for the record, Mr. Bulger," she said, "so it's clear, you're well-served by both counsel in this case, and they are to speak for you in this courtroom at the present time. Do you understand that, sir?"

"Yes sir," Whitey said to the female judge. "Yes."

Judge Casper

IN HIS career as a Boston FBI agent, Morris became known as "Vino," because he liked wine. One night, meeting with his underworld paymasters at the Colonnade Hotel, Vino got so drunk that Flemmi had to drive him home to Lexington in his FBI vehicle, with Whitey following behind to take Stevie back to Boston. That night Morris had brought a tape from the ongoing bugging of Mafia headquarters at 98 Prince Street. Whitey and Stevie kept the tape after Vino passed out; it was the kind of souvenir that might come in handy some day, if everything went south.

Now, under questioning from Fred Wyshak, Morris was describing his new, post-retirement career in Florida.

"Wine consultant, wine educator," he said, without a trace of irony in his voice. "Started primarily as a retail wine clerk, kind of a glorified wine clerk, and over the years I've studied more about wine to the point where I teach staff about wine, I teach it to the public, teach it at a local college."

At the defense table, Whitey continued his doodling, without even cracking a smile.

WHITEY'S FAVORITE FBI agent was, of course, John "Zip" Connolly. Not only were they both from Southie, but they had originally shared the same protector in the federal government—U.S. House Speaker John McCormack of South Boston.

Billy Bulger had grown up as a member of the McCormack political machine in Southie. During Whitey's 1956–65 stint in federal prison, McCormack, first the House majority leader and later the speaker, made sure that Whitey was taken care of. And a few years after Whitey was released, in 1970, "the Director" sent a memo to the Boston office, directing that Whitey be recruited as an informant. The Speaker and J. Edgar Hoover were good friends; they had to be, for Hoover to write a memo on behalf of such a minor hoodlum as Whitey was then, shylocking for Donald Killeen and taking bets on dog races at Wonderland in the afternoons. Dennis Condon reached out to Whitey, but Bulger said he was too preoccupied with the ongoing gang war against the Mullens to take on a new task. His file was closed.

Two years before Hoover wrote on Whitey's behalf, he had gotten another letter from Speaker McCormack, dated Aug. 1, 1968.

"Dear Edgar," it began. "It has come to my attention that the son of a lifelong personal friend has applied to become a special agent of the Federal Bureau of Investigation . . ."

Zip Connolly got back to Boston in 1972, after he captured Cadillac Frank Salemme on a Manhattan street—a gift from two of his corrupt mentors in the Bureau, agents H. Paul Rico and Dennis Condon. They were approaching retirement age, and whatever their future plans, they would need a go-to guy in the Boston office. Who better than a son of Southie like Zip?

Rico and Condon arresting Mafioso Henry Tameleo

Connolly and Morris both arrived at the Boston office in 1972. Morris was assigned to what became C-3, the organized crime squad. In 1975, Zip made another run at Whitey, and succeeded in recruiting him as an informant, supposedly by telling him the Mafia had their own police sources whom they would use to eventually take him down. According to the stories Zip later told, as he tried to create his own myth, he told Whitey, "If they're going to play checkers, we'll play chess."

Before meeting for the first time with Connolly, Whitey cleared it with the hierarchy of the Hill. They were okay with it; they had their own police sources. Johnny Martorano even told him to take care of Connolly.

The first meeting went well. A few months later, Whitey approached Stevie privately, and invited him to a meeting at a coffee shop in Newton with Connolly and Condon, whom Stevie knew from his days as an FBI informant a decade earlier.

Stevie claimed the situation made him nervous; none of his other partners knew he'd been an informant, but now Whitey obviously did. He felt coerced, or so he claimed later, into returning to his old role as a rat.

Stevie was the prize catch, of course. Unlike Whitey, he had a long history with "In Town." They tried repeatedly to entice him into leaving the Hill. He always declined, but he still worked with them, hung with them, and he was the one who could provide usable information about them to the FBI.

Meanwhile, Morris moved to Lexington, also the home of Condon, a Charlestown native and Rico's longtime partner. They drove to work together each day. But soon Morris' "best friend" was Zip. And soon Zip wanted him to meet his neighbor and blue-ribbon informant, Whitey Bulger. Oddly, Zip suggested they meet at Morris' house in Lexington.

"He wanted it to be pleasant surroundings, not the type of surrounding that you would ordinarily meet an informant, in an automobile, possibly in a hotel room, and so forth. He wanted Mr. Bulger to be comfortable, and essentially, he wanted him handled in a manner in which informants typically aren't handled . . . It was more like a social meeting than business."

Later, Morris would meet Stevie Flemmi, with Whitey Bulger. Two informants meeting together, he had never seen anything like that. But they were a "package deal."

One Sunday night strategy session between the killers and the G-men was held at Mrs. Flemmi's house, across the courtyard from the home owned by Senate president William M. Bulger.

"He wasn't at the meeting, no. He did pass through to watch a television show, because he didn't allow television in his home. He just walked through . . . He just looked very uncomfortable, and left the room, watched television, came back out. I don't even think he looked in our direction."

SOON MORRIS was accepting "gifts" from Stevie and Whitey. A bottle of wine here, a silver-plated ice bucket there, and then a case of wine. Zip delivered it to Morris in the basement garage of the federal JFK building, where the FBI had its offices.

"I told him that I did not want to take it and he said, Well, they'll think—meaning Mr. Bulger and Flemmi—will think that you don't trust them, and that if you wanted to give it back, meaning me, I had to do it myself because he wasn't going to do it."

At the time Morris was his supervisor, in addition to his "best friend."

By 1981, the mob was attempting to take over World Jai Alai through John Callahan, an accountant and wannabe gangster. The hostile takeover was not going well. Johnny Martorano had murdered World Jai Alai's owner, Roger Wheeler, but his family still refused to sell out. But no one seemed to be in any danger until one night in the fall of 1981, when Brian Halloran was sitting in an after-hours restaurant in Chinatown, high on cocaine. Suddenly he pulled out a gun and shot the cocaine dealer he was with.

The third person at the table, Jackie Salemme, Frank Salemme's younger brother, dove for cover. Halloran stumbled out the door, leaving behind both his car keys and trademark scally cap.

Halloran was in deep trouble. But he had information, and he went to FBI agents he knew—not Connolly or Morris. He told those agents that before Martorano was brought in, he'd been offered the Wheeler contract. His drinking buddy Callahan made the pitch, with Whitey and Stevie present. That was explosive enough information, but Halloran had more. He said he'd seen Whitey murder a gangster named Louis Litif upstairs at Triple O's in 1979. He said Whitey had a guy at a local cemetery who was burying bodies of murder victims for him, underneath recently interred caskets.

KNOWING THAT Morris had become something of an expert on the Winter Hill Gang, the two agents handling Halloran went to him and inquired about Halloran's status in the gang. He answered noncommittally, and a few days later he ran into Zip Connolly.

"I believe he was at the Master in Public Administration Program at Harvard, and he came in the office one day, and I posed a hypothetical

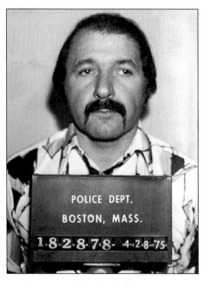

Louis Litif

Brian Halloran

question to him. I asked, is there any way that the Winter people would trust Brian Halloran to do anything?"

> PROSECUTOR FRED WYSHAK: "Did you tell Mr. Connolly what Mr. Halloran was cooperating about?"
>
> MORRIS: "Yes."

A few weeks later, Halloran and Michael Donahue, a guy giving him a ride home after an afternoon of drinking, were shot to death on Northern Avenue in South Boston. In the weeks leading up to the murder, Connolly had filed a number of false 209 reports, saying that any number of underworld figures, including a Charlestown group and the Mafia, were looking to kill Halloran.

> WYSHAK: "Did you understand this was disinformation?"
>
> MORRIS: "Yes."

Halloran was murdered May 11, 1982. On June 2, Morris left Boston for an FBI drug-training session in Glynco, GA. It would be a perfect opportunity for him to spend a few days with his mistress, who was also his secretary. Morris called Zip.

"I asked if he thought that they, meaning Bulger and Flemmi, would spring for an airline ticket to bring her down to Georgia. I remember some time well prior to this Connolly making the statement that, You know, these guys really like you, and if there's anything you ever wanted or needed, to just ask, and I did."

They gave Zip $1,000 cash, which he gave to Morris' girlfriend.

Whitey now owned Morris. But of course, he also owned Connolly. Zip now comported himself more like a flashy, high-rolling wiseguy than a wingtip-wearing G-man. When he retired in 1990, Nick Gianturco, another agent accused of accepting money from the Mob, served as the master of ceremonies at Zip's farewell dinner at Joe Tecce's. He recalled the days when the C-3 squad was "sitting" on the Mafia bugs at 98 Prince Street. The surveillance was taking place in an uncomfortable minivan, and the other agents in the unit, Gianturco said, would always show up dressed casually, for comfort, in sweatsuits. But Zip appeared, he said, in Armani suits, "looking like a member of the Gambino crime family."

It was around this time that the honest agents began calling Connolly "Cannoli." Wyshak asked Morris about Connolly's new lifestyle.

"He was wearing much more jewelry. He was almost showy in terms of the way he dressed, the way he carried himself."

He had bought two homes, in one of the nicest neighborhoods in Southie (from a bookie who was retiring) and a second vacation home in the ritzy Cape town of Chatham. He also had a large boat. He was beginning to think about retirement, and his dream of becoming Boston Police Commissioner. Zip wanted Morris to be his number two.

The job would be delivered by Whitey's brother, the Senate president. Every St. Patrick's Day Billy Bulger hosted a major political roast in South Boston. Morris now sat in the front row with his best friend. Zip had become a prince of the city.

"He had tremendous access across the board to almost everything, including sports events, political figures, and actually for SAC's (special agents in charge), you know, SAC's during inspections there, they're judged on their contacts in the community."

Given his exemplary record, in 1984 Morris was dispatched to Miami to handle an investigation involving a . . . corrupt FBI agent. When he returned to Boston that Christmas, Zip asked him to stop by his posh new digs in Thomas Park. There, he gave Morris a case of wine, and said, "Be careful, there's something in the bottom for you."

It was another $1,000.

Later, Morris would meet Stevie and Whitey at his girlfriend's apartment in Woburn.

"I remember Mr. Bulger was wearing a leather jacket, and out of the leather jacket he pulled an envelope, and he handed it to me, and he said, 'Here, this is to help you out,' and exited."

It was $5,000.

Morris was also taking cash and other gratuities from other "sources."

"I received a loan of $5,000 from one. I also used his condominium

Whitey Bulger

in Florida on two occasions, and during my divorce when I was first separated, I didn't have any place to live. I lived rent-free in a very small efficiency above his garage."

Soon he discovered that one of Stevie's top bookies in Roxbury was being targeted. His phone was going to be tapped. Morris felt he had no choice but to tip Flemmi. If Flemmi were picked up on the wire, he might be indicted, and turn on Morris. On the other hand, if he knew his bookie was a target, he might kill him, and Morris didn't want "another Halloran."

"At this point, I was devastated. I knew I was completely trapped, that I was in so far I could never get out of it. I just—I felt helpless. I just—I didn't know what to do, but I felt awful about everything."

By 1987, he was leaking information to the *Globe* Spotlight team, not just about Whitey's "special relationship" with the FBI, but also about an extortion investigation involving Billy Bulger. After an administrative (rather than criminal) investigation, the FBI learned that Morris was responsible for the leak and suspended him for two weeks without pay.

By now, Morris was desperate to escape Boston. And he did, by applying for any new FBI positions that became open. And, in the inscrutable ways of the federal bureaucracy, Morris continued his career advancement. By the early 1990's, he had been promoted to assistant special agent in Los Angeles in charge of white-collar crime.

Wyshak asked Morris how an agent as dirty as he was could rise so spectacularly through the ranks.

"Because other than this incident with the leaks and their finding that I lacked candor in cooperating with the investigation, my record was spotless."

Spotless. So spotless, in fact, that by 1995 he was at the FBI academy in Quantico, VA, as the "chief of training" for young recruits. In Boston Stevie was under arrest and Whitey was on the lam. One night Morris was working late when he got a call from a "Mr. White."

"He said, essentially, that he wanted me to use my Machiavellian mind to contact my sources at the *Globe* to get them to retract the story about him being an informant, and that if I didn't, I had taken money from him, and if he went to jail, I was, quote, I was coming with him, unquote."

He also mentioned he'd be willing to go one-on-one with Morris "on the box"—a polygraph test. It was the last straw for Morris. Soon thereafter, he went into "full cardiac and respiratory arrest."

"I was just so distraught, and one of my responsibilities was new agents. And here I was, the guy that sometimes was swearing them in, sometimes giving them their credentials and I could remember the Director coming in and giving speeches on integrity, and I just—I couldn't take it anymore. I had to get out."

He retired Dec. 31, 1995. Whitey called Weeks to chuckle about what he'd done to Vino. A couple of years later, Morris found out that Flemmi was talking about the payoffs he and Whitey had made to him. Morris knew how the system worked—he who gets there first gets immunity. He got there first. He kept his pension.

HANK BRENNAN handled the cross-examination. He had done his homework. He immediately pounced on the fact that Morris had repeatedly described himself as "compromised."

"You were corrupt, weren't you, Mr. Morris?"

"Yes."

"Is there a difference between 'compromised' and 'corrupt,' or did you mean the same thing when you said you were compromised?'"

"Same thing."

Then he brought up an almost-forgotten scandal involving Morris and the Boston FBI office. The point was to show that Morris had been corrupt even before he became best friends with Zip Connolly. The feds had been trying to flip a loan-sharking victim to testify against Winter Hill. Ironically, one of the targets was Brian Halloran. The feds needed a witness named Eddie Maiani—Eddie Miami, as he was known.

EDWARD M. MAIANI MBI #174715
DOB 12-29-24 Revere, Mass.
5-4½-150 Brown hair, Brown eyes
Med Comp, Med Build (1964 Photo)
MSBI - PMD # 286

Eddie Maiani

Morris decided that the best way to flip Maiani was to plant what appeared to be a bomb under his car, and then tell him that the Hill was trying to eliminate him as a witness.

"I believe it was my idea. The message was to Mr. Maiani that somebody was out to get him and that something happened that was interrupted."

Brennan asked if he had ever considered the possibility that some of the police and fire personnel responding to the report of a bomb might suffer injuries in their rush to get to the scene.

"I hadn't thought about that," he said. "I just knew it would scare him."

BRENNAN: "Mr. Connolly was not there that night, was he?"

MORRIS: "I don't think so."

THE CROSS-EXAMINATION continued the next day, with Brennan concentrating on the fact that Morris' tip to Zip had led, at least indirectly, to the murders of Halloran and Donahue. After Flemmi was indicted, Morris admitted, he had "panicked." But he said that wasn't the only reason he went to the government to cut himself a deal.

"I didn't want to carry that burden anymore. I wanted to get out from under it."

The questioning was brutal. Wyshak objected time and again, and most of the time, the judge sustained his objections. Unlike, say, Weeks, Morris never fought back.

BRENNAN: "Is your opinion changing of yourself, Mr. Morris?"

MORRIS: "Yeah, my opinion of myself changed quite a while ago."

HE WAS a beaten man. He had been a beaten man for a long time. He admitted to lie after lie after lie. He said he didn't know his nickname was Vino.

"And there were occasions," Brennan said, "at least one, when you needed a ride home from organized-crime figures because you couldn't drive?"

"I believe there is one time." Like so many other witnesses, he sometimes referred to his experiences with Whitey in the present tense, as if they had never ended.

Brennan had him read one preposterous report after another. One, from 1980, concerned the tip on the State Police bug on the Lancaster Street garage in the West End, where Whitey had set up shop. The FBI had been accused of leaking the information, but for once, they were not guilty. Zip Connolly used a FBI-209 report to let Flemmi explain that the information came from a state trooper.

"Source . . . indicated that it was done as a favor, rather than a corrupt act, in view of the fact that the State Police officer and (Flemmi) had known each other and had been friendly since childhood."

And that, apparently, made it all right. Then Brennan began going over informant reports that Connolly had apparently lifted from other agents, and then rewritten so that he could attribute them to Whitey.

One report, from May 2, 1979, listed a different source than Bulger as having "advised that the Sullivan Brothers, Richie and Bobby, from the South End, were the ones who set up Daniel Connolly to be whacked out at the New Market Steakhouse on Southhampton Street on April 29, 1979."

Then Brennan asked Morris to read a report from Bulger from Feb. 19, 1980:

Brennan asked him if he noticed that Connolly had apparently lifted the report about the Sullivan brothers on behalf of his informant.

"I'm not sure I connected the two. I have no memory."

INTO HIS third day of cross-examination, Brennan grew ever more pointed, as he went over old ground, like the 1982 trip his girlfriend made to Georgia with the $1,000 bribe Whitey gave him after the Halloran tip.

"Sir, did you miss your mistress?"

"Yes, I did."

"And that was a relationship you had with your secretary?"

"That's correct."

"While you were married?"

"That's correct."

When he received the $5,000 bribe, Whitey had said he hadn't seen him in a while.

"They missed you, Mr. Morris?"

"I think that phrase was used."

The Report About the Sullivans' Murder Spree that Zip Lifted and Attributed to Whitey

```
BS 92-423
JC/dw
1


           On 2/19/80, BS 1544-OC advised that when Peachy was
"whacked out" on State Street, a guy by the name of Louie LNU
from Revere, who was supposed to be connected to the Laffey
Brothers, set him up to be hit and left via the back door
when the shooting started.  Louie LNU has been over the Mass.
Avenue area and has frequented the Marconi Club on occasion
according to source.  Source advised that she heard from someone
very close to Carmen Tortora that the Sullivan Brothers "whacked
out" Dan Conley over money owed to the late Johnny Stokes by
Red Assad.  Dan Conley was shaking down Assad and the Sullivan
Brothers "whacked" him out at the New Market Steakhouse.  Source
advised she also heard that Tommy Cericola and Frank Russo,
who were murdered in an apartment on Revere Beach, were also
"whacked" out by the Sullivan Brothers in connection with a
drug rip off.  Source advised that Carmen Tortora's girlfriend
told source that Larry Baione himself "whacked" out Chris
Demelio and he was set up by Peter Limone and Richie Gambale.

           THE ABOVE INFORMATION IS SINGULAR IN NATURE AND SHOULD
NOT BE DISSEMINATED OUTSIDE THE BUREAU WITHOUT FIRST CONTACTING
THE WRITER.
```

Exhibit 357-0155

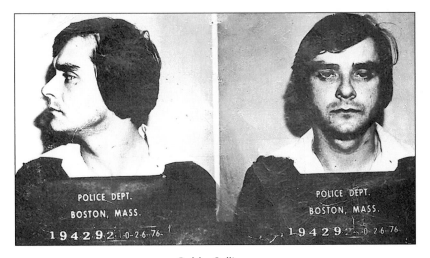

Bobby Sullivan

Dan Connolly

John Stokes

"How did it make you feel that Mr. Bulger missed you, Mr. Morris?"

Then Morris gave the money to his concubine and told her to put it in a separate bank account. This occurred right around the time that Morris was overseeing an investigation of Boston police detectives who were fired, imprisoned and lost their pensions for taking such favors as free meals.

"You saw to it that these men inevitably lost their jobs for what they did?"

"Yeah, it made me sick."

"And you were doing the exact same thing, weren't you?"

"It made me sick, yes."

Brennan asked Morris about his work for various charities, and whether it was related to the guilt he felt about the murders of Halloran and Donahue. Then Brennan asked him if he'd ever reached out to the families of the two dead men to apologize. When he said he would have liked to, Brennan pointed out the Donahues in the victims' row.

Morris turned to them and addressed them directly:

"I don't ask for your forgiveness, but I do want to express my sincere apology for things that I may have done and things that I didn't do. Not a day in my life has gone by that I haven't thought about this. Not a day in my life has gone by that I haven't prayed that God give you blessing and comfort for the pain that you suffered. I'm truly sorry. I do not ask for forgiveness, that's too much, but I do acknowledge it publicly."

It was a poignant moment, which Brennan followed by asking, "Three weeks after those murders, that's when you asked for money for that plane ticket, wasn't it, Mr. Morris?"

"Unfortunately. At that time, I didn't think that they had anything to do with it." Before dying, Halloran had identified his killer as Jimmy Flynn. "I was relieved that it was Flynn."

Patricia Donahue

A few minutes later, Brennan brought up Morris' divorce. Using information obviously supplied by Whitey, Brennan asked if Morris remembered "when you told him that you wanted some help to take care of your problem, which was your wife?"

"Absolutely not."

"Do you remember Mr. Bulger told you that he wouldn't have anything to do with it?"

"Absolutely—there is no such conversation."

At the end, Brennan returned to Morris' penultimate job in the Bureau, in the Los Angeles office, as assistant special agent in charge for white-collar crime, public corruption and government fraud.

"And apparently," Brennan said, "the DOJ found you most fitting to be in charge of public corruption?"

"I think the SAC (special agent in charge) made that decision."

"Something you were well qualified for, weren't you sir?"

"Yes," said Morris, "I think I was."

"I have no further questions, your Honor."

Whitey prosecutors: Brian Kelly, Zachary Hafer and Fred Wyshak Jr.

"He Kept the Drugs Out of Southie"

It was July 2, 2013.

"Your Honor," said prosecutor Brian Kelly, "the United States would call William Shea."

"He may be called," said Judge Denise Casper.

Billy Shea ambled easily to the stand. He was 74 years old, lived in Florida, had for years. He had been the boss of the crew that Whitey Bulger and his sycophants always claimed never existed—the drug organization.

Shea was convicted of an armed robbery in 1970, and had been sent off to MCI-Walpole for seven years. When he was sentenced in 1970,

Billy Shea

Southie was not that much different than it had been at the start of World War II. John McCormack was still the Speaker of the U.S. House, Joe Moakley was the state senator, Billy Bulger was an obscure state rep.

Louise Day Hicks towered over the Town's politics and was about to succeed McCormack in Congress.

Southie High was still segregated. Teenage boys who knocked up their girlfriends were given a choice by the judge—marriage or the Marines. The Killeens still ran the Town's underworld, however shakily, with the muscle of guys like Whitey Bulger and Billy O'Sullivan.

Billy Shea was finally released in November 1977, and it was like coming back to a whole new world. Southie High was in shambles after busing, much of the Town's middle class had decamped to the suburbs. If you impregnated a girl, you no longer had to marry her; in fact it was considered stupid, since you'd be on the hook for child support. Better to let the state provide for the kid via AFDC.

But as a career criminal, the biggest change Shea noticed was the emergence of a new moneyed class in South Boston.

"After I had been home a while, I couldn't help but notice that there was many individuals walking around with rolls of $100 bills large enough to choke a horse, but it appeared to be they had no protection, it appeared to me they were not organized."

So Billy Shea paid a visit to his new friend Jim Bulger. He had a sales pitch for him.

Of course Shea had needed time after his release from prison to really bond with the paranoid, reclusive gang boss. Shea had first returned to his old corner, at Fifth and D Streets, where his Fifth Street Crew was still sullenly resisting Bulger's takeover of the rackets in Southie. "A little tension," as Shea described it. One day Whitey pulled up in his car with another individual, but he didn't speak to Shea.

The next time, Whitey was with Stevie Flemmi—Shea called him by his Southie street name, "Fleming." It was a brief conversation. Whitey said he'd heard good things about Shea. They were feeling one another out. Finally, Bulger reached into his coat pocket, pulled out an envelope, handed it to Shea and said, "Welcome home."

Shea opened it and saw $500 cash.

KELLY: "Did he say why he was giving it to you?"

SHEA: "Holidays, the upcoming holidays."

It was a cheap enough way of building up a little good will with the Fifth Street crew. Plus, Whitey knew Shea wanted to get back to work. Soon he was given a slot on Jack Curran's loan-sharking crew. Shea was ambitious, and he quickly went to Whitey for permission to open a "card room," a safe haven for high-rolling card players to use with the knowledge that they wouldn't be robbed.

"He says, 'Sure, Bill.' And that was it. He didn't charge me anything for opening the card room. I think he was making a sincere effort to—not just myself, but others in Fifth Street Crew, to absorb us, absorb the crew, the entire crew, and he was making inroads."

Eventually, Billy Shea went to Whitey with his idea—getting the Town's drug dealers "in line," as he put it. It could be very lucrative, if every drug dealer in Southie was "in line."

"In other words, they're not organized—they're not mavericks anymore, the day of being a maverick is over, I'm going to absorb them."

"They'd have to pay you?" Kelly asked.

"Well, yeah, that was the basic idea originally," Shea said.

Whitey was all on board, except for one thing.

"He just said he didn't want his name attached to being involved in drugs."

So they worked out a charade, a different kind of "ruse." Once Shea and his crew began rounding up dealers, they'd run to Whitey. But given Whitey's anti-drug reputation, they couldn't tell him why they were being extorted.

"They would say they have a problem and name an individual, maybe myself, maybe someone else in our crew, and he would just say, Hey, they're dangerous people, you got a problem with them, they're my friends, deal with them. . . . You got a problem with them, I don't care what your problem is, deal with them."

Soon Shea was cruising the streets of Southie in his car, looking for drug dealers. He recruited two notorious bad-asses to ride around with him. Freddie Weichel, who would soon go to prison for murder, where he remains to this day, was in the front seat. In the back was Tommy Nee, an even more fearsome name in Southie.

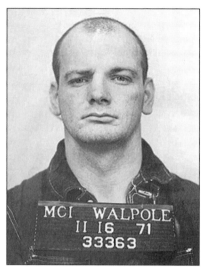

Fred Weichel   Thomas Nee

"We'd pull up, pull them over—'Get in the car.' If they didn't get in, I would explain to them that this was daylight, you notice it's daylight, the next time you see us, it will be nighttime, you won't have a chance to speak to us."

They would get in the backseat. Shea was driving, Weichel was beside him in the front seat. The dealer would have to sit next to Nee, and what he'd immediately notice on the seat, covered with a towel, was an automatic weapon. Intimidation.

"Nee or Weichel wouldn't have to say too much. The criminal element in Boston knew who was dangerous and who wasn't. They knew."

If the dealer seemed mesmerized by the weapon, Shea would tell them, "Don't mind that, it's for a piece of business later on. It was all show, dog and pony."

It was a delicate balance Shea was looking for—"if you intimidated them too much, they just flee. They'll just take off out of the neighborhood, and there goes a nice little revenue stream."

So with his two bad cops in the car, armed, Shea could be the good cop, the good wiseguy.

"I actually wished them a lot of success, great success in their business, but unfortunately the maverick days were over, they would come into our fold or they'd be out of business."

That was the stick. Next came the carrot.

"Coming in with us would give them a lot of benefits, protections. No more would they be subject to being robbed"—except by Shea and Bulger—"or people purchasing their product and not paying. We would give them product that would be equal or better, and our price was lower. But basically it was intimidation."

And it worked, 100 percent of the time. "I don't remember anyone not capitulating. Simple as that."

Over at Triple O's, a 26-year-old cocaine dealer named Joe Tower was very nervous. He'd heard about the shakedowns, and he was extremely concerned, especially about Tommy Nee—"a very bad person, a murderer."

Or, as the wiseguys would say, "capable." A little too capable for Whitey's liking, even though he was on the Bulger payroll. Every few weeks, Whitey would feed Zip more information on Nee—his associates, his hideouts, his automobiles, the license numbers.

Tower was a hustler—he had a couple of auto-body shops, as well as a rock band that occasionally played

Joe Tower

Triple O's. But his main business was cocaine. In fact, Tower was one of Southie's pioneers in the Class B controlled substance that was about to sweep the nation. In addition to playing there, Tower hung out at Triple O's, and he discussed his problems with Kevin O'Neil. It was O'Neil who suggested he meet with Whitey.

A day or so later, Tower was in his house at L and 7th Street when he saw a familiar blue Malibu pull up. It had wire wheels, a vinyl top. Everyone in Southie knew that car—it belonged to Whitey. Whitey was driving, O'Neil was riding shotgun. Tower got in the backseat and explained the situation.

"Yeah," said Whitey, following the script he'd worked out with Shea earlier, "you do have a problem."

Then Whitey asked him about the dimensions of his business.

"I described to him that I had a pretty extensive cocaine business, extending north, south, in every direction."

Whitey then offered Tower a proposition.

"I would like you to hook up with a friend of mine. His name is Billy Shea. If you take Mr. Shea and explain to him what this business is all about, show him the ropes, you will not be bothered."

At this point in his testimony, Kelly asked Tower if he saw James Bulger anywhere in the courtroom.

Tower nodded, pointed and looked his old boss in the eye. "How you doing, Jim?"

Tower then returned to his story.

"I got to admit, they knew nothing about that particular part of the business, the cocaine business, so it was kind of like ground floor."

Then Tower introduced Shea to his clientele. Tower told them their problems were over. No more Tommy Nees shaking them down. Slowly, Tower's customers were "pulled away from me," but he didn't care all that much. Business was too good. They were moving 40 to 70 ounces a week. And that was before the product was cut, with "things like mannitol, inositol. There was different ingredients that could be bought, and double-boiled and made into a particular formula the same color as cocaine. It could be mixed undetected and, in doing so, it gained weight, and weight was money."

The cocaine was coming up from Florida, and they also had a couple of Colombia suppliers out on Commonwealth Avenue. As Tower saw it, the only problem was Billy Shea.

"He had a way of doing things. It was always the tough-guy approach. And I always said, that isn't how you run a business. These people aren't going to work with you like that."

But that's exactly who Whitey wanted running his drug business—wiseguys. He didn't trust the younger generation, guys who hadn't done time, guys who weren't capable. Whitey put more of his plug-uglies onto the payroll, but they weren't allowed to sample the product. Tower handled all the taste-testing.

In the fall of 1983, Tower and Shea were arrested. While awaiting trial, Tower tried to keep the business going, using his brother Tom. But one of his regular customers in Wakefield was in arrears. Tower asked him what the problem was, and he said he couldn't pay, because he'd been stiffed by one of his customers, who said his uncle was a "big wheel."

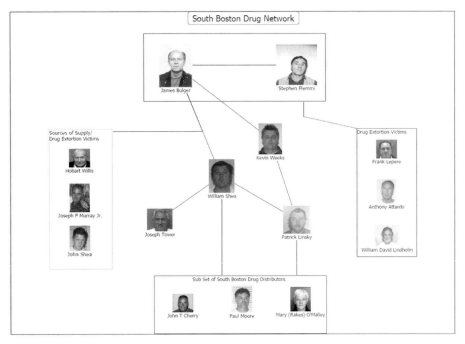

Southie drug chart

Tower told the guy to have his customer call him. He ended up talking to the deadbeat's wife, who told him he wasn't getting anything, and that if he came up there looking to get paid, he'd have serious problems.

"So I told him—her, I said, Listen, it's just the opposite. You have a serious problem."

A while later, she called Tower back. She said he could come up to a roadhouse in Lynn and pick up his money. Tower sent his brother Tom. An hour later Joe Tower got another call, from a guy who said they now had both his brother and the money.

"I says, who's this? He says, Never mind who's this. You got some serious problems and your brother's got some serious problems. I says, again, you got it wrong. I don't think you know who you're dealing with here."

The guy in Lynn threatened to kill Tom Tower. Then he put Tom on the phone. Tom told his brother that the guy and his friends, one of whom was a "triggerman," were threatening to kill him.

"I says, You put him back on the phone again. He put him back on the phone, the gentleman. I told that gentleman that he was a piece of shit and that if he touched my brother, that he was going to be a dead man and, you know, he's going to be getting a phone call. And I hung up on him."

Tower called Billy Shea. Shea called Whitey. Tower waited for the next phone call from Lynn. The guy eventually did telephone Tower. He said he'd been talking to Tom Tower and he says "you're with some guys from South Boston . . . He says you're with some people over there, and those people ain't involved with drugs."

Legends die hard.

"He says that you're with this fellow named 'Boots' and 'Rifleman.' And I says, Listen, you just made a serious mistake. Now you're in serious trouble. I said, there's going to be an army coming over there. So the best thing for you to do is let my brother go, end of story, we're on our way."

Whitey didn't like people using his name. Boots was a nickname—like Paulie McGonagle, he wore boots. He claimed he needed them to hide his shiv, but the reality was, Whitey too was conscious of his height, just like McGonagle, and just like his brother Billy, the Corrupt Midget.

Shea called him back and told him to go down to the Liquor Mart. Whitey, Weeks and Shea were already there. Shea walked over to him and said it's being taken care of. A few minutes later Whitey came up to Tower and said, "Your brother Tom is on his way home. You're all set."

Standing there, Tower asked Shea, what about the money?

"He says, we won't be seeing anybody in Wakefield. We won't be worrying about the money or the roadhouse in Lynn. It's out of our hands. They will be seeing them personally from now on."

A few weeks later, Shea and Tower went on trial. Shea beat the rap, Tower was found guilty and got a "five-year Concord." He did three months behind the wall, a few more across the street at the prison farm, and then a few months in a halfway house on Huntington Ave.

While he was gone, his wife got $1,000 a week, delivered by either Shea or Patty Linskey, another of Whitey's gangsters, who in 1968 had been arrested for murdering a black man on D Street with Kevin O'Neil. Neither was convicted.

After getting out of prison, Tower was still being given $1,000 a week.

"Didn't know where, how or when that was going to come to a stop, but it did."

Patty Linskey called him and told him to come down to Kevin O'Neil's variety store next to Triple O's. There Linskey told Tower he was out.

"I argued, and Mr. O'Neil pulled me back and, Listen, you don't want to do that. But Mr. Linskey said, this was orders from the 'other guy.' The 'other guy' said it was over."

And so it was. Tower now lives in Port St. Lucie, FL where he makes custom guitars for a living. At age 59, he is a luthier.

Jimmy Kearns supplied "gangster grass"

AS TOWER left the witness stand, Whitey's lawyer Jay Carney asked for a sidebar conference.

"My client needs to use the facilities," he whispered to Judge Casper, "and he can't wait until the break."

"Okay," said the judge. "All right."

"It may not be a full break," said Carney. File under, Too Much Information.

AT FIRST, before hooking up with Joe Tower, Shea and his crew were mostly selling grass—really low-quality weed. It was known in Southie as

Joe Tower outside court

"gangster grass." It came from Jimmy Kearns, one of the few survivors of the old Joe Barboza gang. He was tight with Pat Linskey and Tommy Nee, whom Whitey was still trying to get locked up. Kearns' marijuana came in 100-pound bales, and the dealers—not to mention their customers—complained incessantly about it. But they had to buy it.

"Otherwise I would run them out of town," Shea said.

Shea owned a couple of houses on E Street. In one of them, he took the vacant first floor unit, furnished it and then installed timing switches on the lights, to make it look like someone was living there. Then he installed a trap door in the bedroom closet, which led to the basement. Next he walled off a quarter of the cellar, which became "the Vault." At first they stored the marijuana there, and later Joe Tower would use the area to cut up the kilos—the "pizzas," as they called them. After awhile, Shea complained to Whitey about Kearns' gangster grass, and a new source was obtained, from a guy who was bringing in Colombian gold in 50-pound bales. Whitey had to vouch for the new dealer before the paranoid Shea would meet him.

"I never really liked meeting new people," he explained. "The more people that you don't know that's not in your tight-knit circle that have known each other for many, many years, the greater the danger. Not only in the present time, but could be a problem down the road."

In the beginning, Whitey's cut—his "end"—was $4,000 a week. But then he met Joe Tower, and a new world opened up. Cocaine.

"Marijuana is bulky, it's hard to store, it's difficult to store, it's difficult to move. But cocaine—much smaller and very easy to move, and plus the profit margin, the cost of the product or the goods versus the end result in the sale, the profit margin was much larger."

Soon Whitey's end was up to $6,000 a week, then $8,000, and eventually $10,000. But then Shea got some bad news. His Colombia suppliers were feeling the heat. They were pulling out. They gave Shea three weeks' notice, not much time to secure a new supply. He went to Whitey, who told him not to worry. They'd found a guy in Charlestown.

What had happened was that Joe Murray of Charlestown, probably the biggest marijuana importer on the East Coast, if not in the entire nation, had taken over an abandoned warehouse on D Street as a marijuana storage house. D Street was in Southie. Whitey was not consulted. Whitey was not paid "rent." Whitey was not happy. Soon the police got a "tip" about the warehouse, but not before Whitey had warned Joe Murray to clear his guys out of there.

A few days later, Zip Connolly filed an FBI-209 about the incident, the theme of which was a familiar one. Whitey was keeping the drugs out of Southie.

```
BS 245F-1
JC/sct
1.

          On 4/7/83, BS 1544-TE advised that the boat that
was grabbed by the Coast Guard a couple of days ago formerly
belonged to Billy Rea, who sold it to the people who currently
own it.  Source advised that Billy Rea currently owns a huge
steel hulled fishing trawler which cost over 1 million dollars
and which was recently used to transport bales of "grass" from
the mother ship.  This is the same grass which was seized at
the "D" Street warehouse.

          Source advised that the Joe Murray crew are up
tight and are extremely anxious to find out who ratted on them.

          Source advised that the Murray crew are also
concerned that Whitey Bulger is upset with them over their
storing the grass in his town.  Bulger supposedly got word
through Pat Nee to the Charlestown crew that he is upset
and that cops that they do business with in the booking and
loansharking think that the South Boston crew had a piece
of the "action".
```

FBI marijuana report

That was the beginning of Whitey's relationship with Murray, which Murray was always trying to end, until he finally did a few years later, with a $500,000 payment. But at this point, Whitey needed cocaine, and Murray was willing to supply it. Pat Nee, like Murray an ardent Irish nationalist, would be Whitey's liaison, his buffer, to the Charlestown crew. A few days later, Whitey told Shea that they were going to meet the new cocaine supplier, at Pat Nee's house, the Matterhorn. Shea was told to bring $100,000 in cash, and Whitey brought $75,000. They got out of the car and then Shea got cold feet about going up the stairs into the house.

"I did a lot of time, I'm a little paranoid. I said, 'Who's upstairs?' He says Pat Nee. See, Jim was not really the connection. Pat Nee was with the Charlestown guy. Who cares? All I know is I wasn't going up the house. I said no Jim, you bring him down. At that point, I could still reason with him. Our background was we'd both done a little bit of time, so we both know the paranoia that might set in, and that night the paranoia set in. I said, no bring him down. Not a demand, I didn't talk to Jim like that. I said, bring him down."

He brought Joe Murray down. Shea gave him the $175,000, and the cocaine—"the product"—was handed to one of the other guys. Shea never, ever touched the cocaine himself. His job was collections, and cutting up the pie, making sure Whitey got his end. Shea insulated himself. It was a lesson he learned from Whitey.

"One of the things he schooled me in pretty good at the beginning was to create buffers. I basically was his buffer to the endeavor, and of course I created buffers with trusted associates so they would take the heat before I did. And I learned to stay away from the product. I was never there at the product."

Murray sold a quality product, or at least compared to what had previously been available in Southie. Shea had come a long way from the days of "gangster grass." With Tower on the shelf, Patty Linskey was his right-hand man. Two wiseguys—just the way Whitey liked it. And business was booming.

"I would say close to $100,000 a week at the time." Shea glanced over at Bulger. "I'm thinking Jim is looking at me thinking, you son of a bitch, you made that kind of money and I got that end."

Whitey looked up from his legal pad and chuckled.

Prosecutor Kelly asked Shea to identify "the other guy."

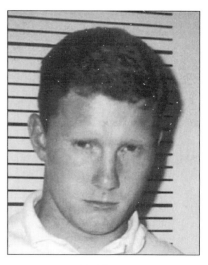

Red Shea

"Yes, I can identify him, he's the young fellow there with the green shirt, I believe it's green."

In the mid-1980's, they heard about a new "rogue" dealer in the Town. John "Red" Shea, a boxer in a "boxing town," as Shea put it. No relation to Billy, but he liked the kid. Red admired a diamond-encrusted bracelet Billy had bought with his "end," and Billy promised his young namesake that if he won a big fight, he'd buy him the same bracelet, minus the diamonds. Red won, and Billy delivered. Now Red was selling some "very high grade cocaine" out of a few clubs.

Shea and Linskey called him in for a meeting.

"We weren't going to hurt him, we just wanted to bring him into the fold. I said Red, two things: you shouldn't have done what you did, if I told Jim, you'd be in trouble, because obviously at this point he's a maverick, he's not kicking in to anybody. But second, I wanted his connection because the cocaine he was bringing in was very, very high quality, solid rock shale. And I would want to get my hands on that. And so he capitulated pretty quick. He wanted to be a quote-unquote 'gangster,' John 'Red' Shea. Unfortunately, he was young. Jim, I think, impressed him, you know, seeing Jim and the rest of the gang. He wanted to be a gangster."

He ended up doing 12 years when he refused to cut a deal to testify against his colleagues in the gang who had turned out to be the biggest rats of all. In the end, Red Shea acted more like a gangster than most of the rats he'd looked up to so much. When Red Shea finally got out of prison, he wrote a book about the South Boston underworld. He called it *Rat Bastards*.

At the beginning of 1986, Billy Shea was ready to cash in his chips. He had money, more money than he'd ever dreamed of. He'd already had one photo finish with a grand jury, and figured he had to be on the "radar screen."

So he broached the subject with Whitey. They'd always had a good relationship, no threats, no muscle, etc. So Shea made the pitch to Whitey—the pie would be bigger, he wasn't looking for a pension. Whitey said no, it'll fall apart, why do you have to leave when it's running "smooth as a sewing machine?" Bulger was getting agitated, so Shea let it slide for awhile. He figured he'd show him that the business could run without him—after all, why were they paying all these "buffers" if they couldn't handle the operation?

He took off for Florida. A few weeks later Whitey called.

"Jim says it's all falling apart, ba-be, ba-be, ba-be, it's falling apart. I told you it would fall apart. I told you it would fall apart. You can't just go off to Florida like that and think you're retired."

Shea came back, was read the riot act, put out a few fires and then took off again. This time when he called from Boston, Whitey was pissed.

"He said, 'If you don't come up, I'll come down there.' I didn't take that as a threat, just that his patience was running out."

Was it ever. When Shea returned to Boston this time, Whitey didn't want to meet him at his house, the way he always had. This time Whitey ordered him to come down to Triple O's. He took Patty Linskey with him and they sat down with Whitey.

"His reply this time, first time ever, he threatened me. He threatened me in words. He said, quote—I'm sure he remembers it because I remember it real clear, the first time he ever threatened me—he says, 'You remember what happened to Bucky Barrett?'"

No expression from Whitey at the defense table. He was just continuing to write—or doodle—on his legal pad.

"You know, I wasn't even upset that he said that. What was more upsetting, he embarrassed me in front of Patrick."

Kelly asked him how he interpreted the Bucky Barrett reference.

"Hey, I took it as 'Bucky Barrett is among the missing.' I took it as a threat, and it was the first time he ever did that, and it changed my perception of Jim Bulger just like that . . . I'm feeling embarrassment. I'm also looking at a guy that I thought I knew for many years and he's threatening me like, you know, You'll do as I say or I'll whack you, basically. So I started looking at him in a completely different light.

Pat Linskey

"I told him—I said, 'Are you threatening me, Jim?' He didn't answer at that point. I said, 'Because I don't respond good with threats.' I didn't mean I was going to do something to him, I meant, you know, fucking— threats is—I don't respond well to them. I'll do the opposite. I do that most of my life when people threaten me, I do the opposite."

Then he got up from the table and left with Linskey, still embarrassed that Pat had heard him dressed down. He went home, cleaned up a few loose ends and returned to Florida, then came back to Boston a few weeks later. Whitey hadn't even called him this time, he just came home. He figured maybe Whitey was getting used to not having him around.

But then one night he heard a knock on his front door. When he opened it he saw Whitey—and Kevin Weeks and, even more ominously, Stevie Fleming, as Shea called him.

"He said he needed to talk to me," Shea recalled. "Well, I found that odd. Whenever we talked, almost all these years, he didn't want anybody around when him and I were talking, so he wants to talk to me with two other individuals, one of them being a very, very dangerous person, just as dangerous as Jim."

Shea said he'd be a moment, then ran upstairs and got a gun—for the first time ever, he was taking a gun to a meeting with Whitey. He went outside with them and got in the car—in the backseat, with Flemmi.

"I probably wouldn't have got in the front. I know the car routine."

They didn't drive far, to the Seventh Street side of the D Street projects, which were being remodeled. Nobody was living in them. It was totally deserted.

"Not as comfortable as my home, or even as comfortable as Triple O's."

Shea and Whitey got out of the car and walked into the empty courtyard. Weeks and Flemmi remained in the car. Flemmi yelled after him, "I wish you'd reconsider." There were several doorways they could have talked in, away from the elements, but Whitey wanted to walk down the cellar steps.

"Now, I don't know how many people are familiar with housing projects, but the cellar steps are like a coffin. You walk down the cellar steps, the deeper you go, there's the concrete reinforcement built around those stairs. By the time you hit the bottom of the stairs, you're in a pretty well-enclosed area. That's what really got me very, very paranoid, very paranoid."

Whitey was in front of him on the stairs, but Shea somehow maneuvered around him.

"Jim may recall, he may not even have picked up on it, but I'm sure he did—I got in front of him and turned so my back was at the cement wall, so there would be nobody coming from my backside."

Whitey was aggravated, but Shea was concentrating on his hands. He always carried a knife, but that was in his boot, which meant he'd have to reach for it. As a convicted felon, he couldn't legally carry a firearm, so he seldom carried any weapon on his person other than the knife.

"So I was looking at his hands to make sure they didn't move any-where, and I was looking over his shoulder to make sure I don't see Stevie's head pop up. . . . If he makes a move, he's going with me. That's basically my state of mind at the time: Jim, if you make a move on me, you're gone, because I know I'm gone if Stevie shows up at the top of the stairs."

They kept talking, even though Shea found it difficult to concentrate while trying to keep his eyes on both Whitey's hands and the top of the stairs.

"He surprised me. We talked back and forth. He mentioned trust. Trust. That's what I remember. Don't forget, I'm down there, you know, my heart's beating a little bit. I'm focusing on him, but I'm very nervous. I know there's other people with him. I know that if it went bad, I'd be gone, I'd be left there."

Shea was wondering what "trust" meant.

"Is he thinking I'll be a loose end? I pointed out to Jim, Don't forget, I took a fall in '83—this is very important—I took a fall in '83, the busi-ness was going full tilt then, I didn't say anything. Trust. It isn't greed, because I'm getting a good piece of the pie. So it isn't greed. He still wants me to stay. If it was greed, he'd say, See ya later, Bill. So it had to be trust."

Then Whitey suddenly relaxed. The tension went out of his face.

"He said, 'Let's get the hell out of here' and we walked up the stairs. We get to the top of the stairs and we're talking and he sort of refers to chicanery. A different word, but it's chicanery. He's referring to skim-ming. And I pointed out that it's been a few years since I even seen the product. I never touched the product, so how could I skim the product? Things like that."

They walked back to the car, where Stevie and Weeks were still sitting.

"He asked me if I wanted a ride. I said, 'No, I can walk.'"

And that was it. The prosecution was finished with Shea. The judge looked at Carney and said, "Cross-examination?"

Carney turned to Shea on the witness stand and said, "Thank you, Mr. Shea. I have no questions, your Honor."

The lawyers then approached the sidebar, and Carney addressed the judge.

"For posterity, I have a fulsome cross-examination, and I believe the prosecutors expected me to use it. And when they asked me how long I expected to go, I, with sincerity, told them I did expect to go quite a bit."

Whitey, it appears, pulled the plug on the cross. He couldn't expect any more positive testimony from any other prosecution witness. The judge sent the jury home for the five-day Independence Day break.

South Boston Liquor Mart

It was July 25, 2013, the 29th day of the trial.

Zach Hafer, the prosecutor, said: "The United States calls Kevin O'Neil."

"Good morning, sir," said the judge.

He lumbered up to the stand, well over 300 pounds. He looked at Whitey and said, "Good morning, Jim."

Every mob needs a Kevin O'Neil, a moneyman, someone who "launders" the dirty cash, whose job it is to ensure that everyone has a reportable, taxable income, just the requisite number of W-2s and 1099s to show the Internal Revenue Service every April. And that was O'Neil's job. Like most of Whitey's crew, he'd ended up in prison after the boss fled, but not for long. As soon as he began to cooperate, O'Neil was out the door, into a Lexus SUV, with his two daughters weeping.

Kevin O'Neil

Definitely not in stature, but in bulk, Kevin O'Neil was the biggest rat in Whitey's barn.

He'd started off as a street thug—in 1968, he'd been arrested for murder in a race riot after the slaying in Memphis of Dr. Martin Luther King, Jr.

Eventually, he got off—"I got a nolle prosequi," he would later explain to the judge. His lawyer was William M. Bulger. He wanted that made clear to the jury. But that would be later in the day, after he had already testified.

Hafer went over his early life, dropping out of South Boston High, after which he went to work, having "a variety of jobs, mostly in women's clothing."

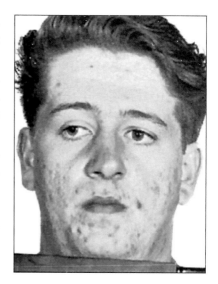

Kevin O'Neil, 1968

That produced some tittering in the courtroom, the thought of Kevin O'Neil in women's clothing. He worked at the Transit Café at 28 Broadway, in the Lower End, when it was owned by Donald Killeen, Whitey's underworld boss. Killeen was murdered in Framingham in 1972. Killeen and his two brothers had owned the ginmill, which was quickly sold off to three other brothers, the O'Neil's. They renamed it Triple O's and "converted the second floor to a function room later on."

The function room was where Whitey conducted many of his shakedowns. It was a dreary place, as Michael Solimando described it. Brian Halloran claimed to have seen Louis Litif murdered there back in 1979.

Soon Whitey Bulger was on Triple O's payroll—as a no-show. It was like his old courthouse janitor's job, except that now he was a private-sector no-show. Whitey didn't actually do anything at Triple O's except hang around and wait for his people to bring him somebody to take upstairs to the function room to extort.

PROSECUTOR HAFER: "Why was he on the payroll?"

O'NEIL: "He asked."

HAFER: "Why didn't you tell him no?"

O'NEIL: "I didn't think it was smart."

Hafer asked O'Neil if he knew of Whitey's reputation.

"He wasn't a guy to fool with," O'Neil said.

Back in 1977, when the New York Mafia sent some guys up to the garage in Somerville to try to recover money that was owed to one of their bookies, O'Neil had been one of the dozens of Winter Hill hoods and associates who were told to go over to the garage and mill around, to deter the New Yorkers from trying to collect. It worked, and it was apparently O'Neil's only visit to Marshall Motors.

He also owned an appliance store, South Boston Households. That was where John Hurley stopped by in May 1982 to tell Whitey that he'd spotted Brian Halloran at the Port Café over on Northern Avenue. There was later testimony that Zip got his appliances for free at South Boston Households, a charge Connolly described as "an abject lie."

Around this same time, in the late 1970's, O'Neil hired Kevin Weeks as his bouncer. Stevie Flemmi started hanging out there at Triple O's as well. In 1999, along with Kevin Weeks, O'Neil was indicted on charges of money laundering, extortion and various RICO counts. He got a year and a day in prison and "had to wear a bracelet for quite a while."

He also had to forfeit Triple O's, some cash and what he called "the package store"—the South Boston Liquor Mart.

As time went on in the 1980's, O'Neil began to collect "rent" from some of the gang's bookies, especially Dick O'Brien. O'Neil just confirmed what the wheelchair-bound bookie had earlier told the jury.

"He'd actually come looking for me. It's not that I wanted to . . . I really didn't want to take them, he just didn't want to go over there because Stevie scared him."

In January 1984, his old bouncer Kevin Weeks asked him to come over to a new liquor store the gang had acquired, Stippo's. Weeks would later plead guilty to extortion in the way he

Stippo Rakes

and Whitey and Stevie had obtained the liquor store—he had pulled a gun on its owner, Stippo Rakes.

It should have been a great package store. For one thing, it was the only place in Southie that had free parking—nine parking spaces, right on Old Colony Avenue, between the two housing projects. But Stippo had gotten a few anonymous death threats after he opened the store just before Christmas in 1983, and his family had panicked.

Stippo's sister, Mary O'Malley, who was in the Bulger drug organization, told Kevin Weeks and Whitey that her

Mary Rakes O'Malley, Stippo's sister

brother was interested in selling. They offered $100,000 cash. But before the deal could close, Whitey and Weeks ran into the package-store owner who'd been making the threats. Whitey told him to knock it off, and word got back to Stippo that his problems were over. He began to get cold feet. But Weeks and Whitey threatened Stippo and the deal was consummated.

For the rest of his life, Stippo would claim the store was extorted from him. But when called before grand juries, he would lie. Eventually he was convicted of perjury and placed on probation. Whitey's trial was going to be Stippo's revenge. He was on the government's witness list. He commissioned one of the courtroom artists to do a painting for him, a profile of Whitey on the right, and on the left, a profile of his brother Billy, with the caption underneath, "I've got your back."

But after Weeks' vehement denial that he'd extorted Stippo, and the fact that Flemmi was apparently going to say much the same thing when he took the stand, the feds decided to drop Stippo from their witness list.

That was on a Tuesday. On Wednesday afternoon, Stippo's body was found in suburban Lincoln, his car a few miles away in a McDonald's parking lot in Waltham. For a few hours, it was a national news story—Bulger witness slain before testifying. Soon, however, it was clear that the murder had nothing to do with the trial. Police arrested a convicted scam artist named William Camuti who'd apparently owed Stippo a large amount of money in a failed real-estate deal.

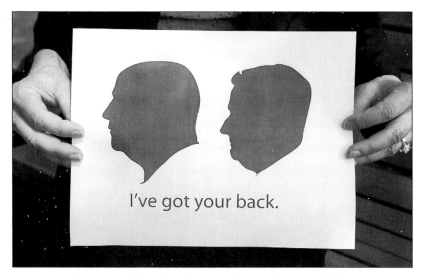

Stippo's profiles of the brothers Bulger, Whitey and Billy

Stippo had been looking forward to seeing O'Neil testify; he called him "Turtleneck Pants" for the fact that he wore his trousers so high, in an effort to hide his gigantic belly. But it was not to be, and there was nobody smirking at O'Neil as he began to explain his long connection with the liquor store.

At first, he just ran the place for them; it was one of his unspoken duties, like Whitey's weekly paycheck from Triple O's. O'Neil whitewashed the wall and then had a giant green shamrock painted on it. The store was

William Camuti

renamed the South Boston Liquor Mart. By 1986, Whitey, Weeks and Stevie wanted to cash out of their minimal investment.

O'Neil brought in a partner, Gordon McIntyre, and they paid $300,000, which they thought included the business, the inventory and the land. But had they really bought the land, Hafer asked.

"There's the question," O'Neil said. "We thought we did, but it ended up we didn't. We paid rent. We had a misunderstanding. We thought we were getting the building too."

As O'Neil well knew, these were not the kind of people you could have a civil disagreement with. He and his partner began paying "rent" on the property they had believed they'd bought. Every year they paid each of the three "owners"—Whitey, Kevin Weeks and Mary Flemmi, Stevie's mother—$7,700.

In addition, O'Neil found himself with three new employees on the South Boston Liquor Mart payroll—Whitey, Weeks and Stevie Flemmi.

HAFER: "Why were they on the payroll?"

O'NEIL: "They asked to be."

HAFER: "Why didn't you just tell them no?"

O'NEIL: "Again, it would be stupid."

He paid each of them $500 a week—as no-shows. Not only that, but certain customers expected deep discounts, among them the Boston office of the FBI. They always bought the liquor for their office Christmas parties at the South Boston Liquor Mart.

"Finest liquor store in the Commonwealth," Zip Connolly joked at his FBI retirement dinner in 1990. A few moments earlier, he'd been given a bottle of wine as a gag gift by Diane Kottmyer, who had succeeded Jeremiah O'Sullivan as chief of the Organized Crime Strike Force.

"John," she said, "they wanted me to say that the bottle came courtesy of South Boston Liquors, but I won't say that."

Kottmyer is now a Superior Court judge in Massachusetts.

In December 1989, a year before Kottmyer joked with Zip about the Mob package store, Whitey decided he wanted to use the Liquor Mart as his piggybank yet again. And he really was going to sell the property, for $400,000. This time all the money would go to Whitey—he'd bought out his two "partners" for a total of $40,000.

Earlier, Whitey had summarily told O'Neil that he now had to buy the property, and O'Neil had to scramble to find a bank that would loan him the money. When O'Neil finally had a deal in place, Whitey called him back.

"He just didn't want to see somebody else make the money instead of him."

So Whitey had decided he would take the mortgage back. O'Neil's new payment would be $4,672.96 a month, or about $56,000 a year, compared to the $23,000 annual payments he had been making in rent.

Whitey Bulger fled Boston in December 1994. O'Neil and his partner continued to write him the monthly $4,672.96-a-month checks, which were dutifully deposited in his bank account, until March 13, 1997.

"Why did you keep paying?" Hafer asked him.

"I believed," said O'Neil, "that he was coming back."

NEXT HAFER asked him about the extortion of Southie businessman Ray Slinger. He had somehow crossed Kevin O'Neil in a business deal. He was therefore "ripe for extortion," as Stevie Flemmi would say. Whitey told O'Neil to bring Slinger upstairs to the function room at Triple O's.

O'Neil remained downstairs in the bar, but later saw Slinger when he came back down. His demeanor? "Shaken."

A couple of weeks later, Whitey told O'Neil to bring Slinger back to Triple O's. This time Slinger brought his secretary with him. She remained downstairs in the bar with O'Neil while her boss went upstairs.

Next, O'Neil said, "I heard somebody yell 'gun,' and what transpired, I don't know. But by the time I ran up the stairs, I guess Ray Slinger had a gun."

In the function room, Whitey now had Slinger's gun, and Weeks had Slinger pinned up against the wall. Whitey ordered O'Neil to leave his own bar. Slinger was then told to stand on a tarp that was lying on the floor. Whitey put Slinger's own gun to his head and told him that if he were shot in the head, no one would ever know because all the blood would be drain onto the tarp and could be easily cleaned up.

Hafer asked if he observed Slinger's demeanor when he left Triple O's the second time. Again O'Neil said, "Shaken."

Two weeks later, Whitey told O'Neil to go to Slinger's real-estate office and pick something up.

"He had an envelope for me."

O'Neil delivered the envelope to Whitey. Then he got his gumption up.

"I said, 'I could lose my license here.'"

And Bulger replied, "You could lose your life."

A few minutes later, after a sidebar conference with the judge, O'Neil was allowed to tell the jury that the 1968 murder charges against him had been dismissed—"that's really important," he explained to the judge. Then he waddled out of the courthouse and into a sea of cameramen and photographers.

Stippo Rakes was no longer around to savor the moment. But if he had been, he'd have enjoyed learning that winding up with the South Boston Liquor Mart hadn't turned out to be the bonanza that either Stippo or Turtleneck Pants had once dreamed of.

The Rat Files

Whitey and his lawyers insisted to the bitter end that he was not a rat. The evidence said otherwise. Stevie Flemmi at least didn't bother to deny anything; of course he had at first, down in Plymouth, when he was locked up with Frank Salemme and John Martorano. He'd said that Wimpy had been the feds' real rat—until Salemme pointed out to him that the reports continued after Wimpy in January 1967.

Even after the trial was over, Whitey was still writing letters, denying the obvious. In late June, though, the prosecutors did a huge document dump—dropping all of both Whitey and Stevie's FBI informant files. Many of them had been in evidence earlier, but having everything out there, on the public record, that was a first.

The documents even included records about Whitey before he officially became an informant. In this one, from June 1965, a female informant tells the FBI that the newly released ex-con claimed to be going straight:

> Informant stated taht she was at Dorgan's Restaurant in South
> Boston during June of 1965, and WHITEY BULGER came to her table
> and introduced himself. He told her that he knew her husband,
> Daniel Herd at the U.S. Penitentiary in Lewisburg, Pennsylvania.
> She stated that BULGER showed her callouses on his hands and
> stated he was working on construction and that he planned
> on going straight as he owed it to his family, all of whom
> were loyal to him when hewas in prison.
>   in

Exhibit 355-00268

But not long afterward, Whitey found himself a predicament common in South Boston back in those days.

> Informant advised she receved a telephone call from WHITEY
> BULGER who stated that he was tired of working but apparently
> would continue to work in spite of it. He told her the reason
> he was calling was because he had a girl in trouble and wanted
> to know if she knew of the name of an abortionist fix this
> girl. She stated he was very upset about this girl being
> in trouble and was desperate.

Exhibit 355-0268

No follow-up on what happened.

DURING THE trial the prosecutors went over many of the smoking-gun FBI-209's—the attempts by Whitey to blame Brian Halloran's impending murder on anyone but himself, or the finger-pointing at the "bad Cubans" before John Callahan was killed in Florida and his personal belongings dumped in Little Havana.

But, with Zip as his FBI amanuensis, Whitey used the FBI-209s to settle any number of all scores, no matter how small. If Whitey didn't like somebody, he would plant information, true or otherwise, it didn't matter, that his enemy was, say, a cocaine user, or an embezzler, or even just a corrupt politician.

For example, consider John E. Powers of South Boston, the first Democrat Senate president in Massachusetts since the Civil War. Later he became clerk of the Supreme Judicial Court, Suffolk County, which gave him power to hire and fire in the Boston courthouses.

He fired Whitey from his no-show job. Once Billy became Senate president, Powers had his salary and those of his aides frozen. At one point

Powers confronted Billy at a party and asked him why he and, especially, his aides with young families were being made to suffer because of the firing of a gangster.

According to Powers, Billy Bulger pointed out that Powers' wife was on the Senate payroll, and he hadn't fired her.

"Are you comparing my wife to your brother?" Powers asked.

Still, though, Whitey wanted to put something into the permanent file, as it were, damaging Powers:

```
BS 194C-215
JC/mmh
1
_.

          On January 29, 1987, BS 1544-TE advised that years
ago, a cop by the name of PHIL DOHERTY sold the bar exam to
several people including former Senate President JOHN POWERS.
Both POWERS, who is the current clerk of the Massachusetts Supreme
Judicial Court and DOHERTY, who is a key aide to Mayor FLYNN,
are supposed to be nervous about the current "exam" case in
Federal Court.  Source stated that both DOHERTY and POWERS were
"rogues".

          Source stated that the old MULLIN gang broke into
POWERS' house on "M" Street in South Boston years ago, and took
out a safe containing $250,000.00 in cash.  Source advised that
POWERS never reported the robbery!
```

Notice how many knocks Whitey gets in there. Powers is a "rogue." So is the aide for Ray Flynn—the mayor who refused to appoint Zip Connolly police commissioner. And Powers is accused of having huge amounts of cash left over from his legislative career, so much that he can't report it to the police when it's stolen by the Mullens, most of whom are by now dead or have moved on.

Sometimes Whitey could manage a turn of phrase—a counterfeiter is described as "half-a-nitwit," feds are discovered on someone's tail because "they're too clean-cut to be Boston cops." One aspiring hood "thinks he's Dutch Schultz." But even that one has a zinger for an old foe. Out of nowhere, Whitey accuses the Quincy cop who developed John McIntyre as an informant of now "protecting" the young Dutch Schultz.

Some of the 209s are chilling in retrospect. This one from 1987 concerns the search for a young woman:

```
BS 92A-2557
JC/dg

                                1
                                ‾


          On November 17, 1987, BS 1544-TE advised that the
world around South Boston is that FRANCES "PRANNY" MANSFIELD
was murdered over a drug beef.  Source advised that MANSFIELD
was involved with a young crew from KELLY'S CORK and BULL
RESTAURANT and she supposedly "mushed" them for a couple of
kilos of coke.  Source advised that the Irish Mob in South
Boston is reaching out to find out who did the murder; not
for ·retribution, but because they want to know who would
be capable of killing a woman.
```

This was more than two years after Whitey had strangled Deb Hussey. So he knew of at least one guy in Southie who was "capable" of killing a woman.

Whitey didn't get around to murdering Bucky Barrett until 1983. But as early as 1980, he was practically salivating to Zip Connolly over how much wealth Bucky controlled:

```
BS 91-8556
JC:po'b
1
‾
          On 6-25-80, BS 1544-TE advised that the"word on
street" is that two police officers, a Medford Sergeant
named Doherty and an MDC Police Captain named Jerry Clemente,
were "in" on the Depositors Trust score.  The setup guy is
supposed to be "Bucky" Barrett who, in turn, is supposed to
have brought in other unknown help.

          The talk is that Barrett has control over the
majority of the gold and diamonds.  There is supposed to be
over 80 pounds of gold.
```

Exhibit 356-0095

Sometimes Whitey planted pure disinformation in his rat files. For instance, as Larry Baione was recorded on the FBI wiretaps of his social club on North Margin Street lauding Whitey and Stevie as two guys who "can straighten a thing out," i.e., handle a murder, Whitey dictated this to Zip about the bugging of Mafia headquarters in the North End:

```
          It should be noted that the current Title III operations
have established two indisputable facts:

     A.   that source is not a "hit man" for Jerry Angiulo
          as has been contended.
```

Exhibit 355-00167

But Whitey had taken part in several hits as the Winter Hill Gang wiped out Indian Al Angeli's gang—as a favor for the Mafia, a favor that netted the Hill $50,000. But Whitey didn't need that out in the public domain. That was another one of his cherished myths—that he was the one guy who stood up to the dreaded "Eye-talians," as Jimmy Carter used to say. He was the guy who killed Mafia, not his own.

More nonsense, of course. When the police started digging up the six bodies Whitey had secretly buried, with three of the four male victims' skeletons, they discovered claddagh rings—an Irish symbol of love and friendship. (A fourth claddagh ring on a Whitey victim—Michael Donahue—was taken off his body by his widow Patricia, who wears it to this day.) Whitey killed more of his own than he did Italians. And mostly his victims weren't flashy high-living mobsters, they were near-destitute tailgaters. The cops never did find dental records on Tommy King and Paulie McGonagle—they were apparently too poor to afford trips to the dentist.

THE MAFIA was much on Whitey's mind, of course. Red Assad was a South End mobster of Lebanese descent. Whitey dictated this report to Zip Connolly on Red:

```
BS 183-84
JC/dw
1
‗

        On 11/13/79, BS 1544-TE advised that in a recent
conversation with RED ASSAD, ASSAD had advised that LARRY
ZANNINO had told him that DOMINIC ISABELLA, FRANKIE SALEMME
(currently incarcerated at the Medfield State Hospital),
and JOHNNIE CINCOTTI had recently been inducted into the LCN.
Source advised that ASSAD seemed to be bitter about it for some
reason and made the statement that no one is closer to LARRY
ZANNINO than himself.  Source believed he was referring to
the fact that he cannot be made a member due to the fact
that he is not of Italian parentage.
```

Exhibit 356-0200

Red Assad

When he was on the verge of being discontinued as an informant in 1980, Whitey had a four-hour sitdown in an East Boston hotel with new Boston Special Agent in Charge (SAC) Larry Sarhatt. First he laid on his Jimmy Cagney rap very thick:

> Informant's intention to help the FBI stems from the favorable treatment received by his family from SA PAUL RICO after SA RICO was responsible for his incarceration. His family indicated to him that SA RICO was such a gentleman and was so helpful that he, Informant, changed his mind about his hate for all law enforcement. Additionally, he has a close feeling towards SA JOHN CONNOLLY because they both grew up in the same neighborhood in Boston and had the mutual childhood problems, as well as his deep hatred for La Cosa Nostra.

Exhibit 355-00190

Then, the traditional he-kept-the-drugs-out-of-Southie rap:

> Additionally, another purpose for this meeting was to be sure that Informant is fully aware that the MSP are convinced beyond a reasonable doubt that he is an Informant of the FBI and his life could be in jeopardy. Informant also related that he is not in the drug business and personally hates anyone who does; therefore, he and any of his associates do not deal in drugs.

Exhibit 355-00192

STEVIE FLEMMI'S 209s are much more substantive. He tells stories that aren't necessarily self-serving, just good gossip, like the time in 1983 when he reported that Mafia underboss Jerry Angiulo had "whispered" to him that then Police Commissioner Joe Jordan "owed him a big favor."

Again, no follow-up. Zip was a stenographer, not an interrogator.

When Angiulo was finally arrested in 1983, Stevie warned that his jailers might have a problem:

```
BS 183A-84 (SUB B)
JC:rap
1.


          On 4-17-84, BS 955-TE advised that the ANGUILOS
are attempting to obtain a list of prospective jurors from
the upcoming trial under the guise of preparing a jury profile
but what they actually want the list for is to see if they
can Reach someone on the list.  Source advised that they
will "move" a juror if they get the chance and JERRY ANGUILO
knows from experience as they had a female relative of
FRANKIE SALEMME on the RED KELLEY ARMORED CAR CASE and
ANGUILO was acquitted.  Source advised that JERRY ANGUILO
is "uptight" lately and was so upset with JOE BALLIRO
that he spit in his face.  Source added that JERRY ANGUILO
will corrupt the entire staff at the Charles Street Jail
if he gets the chance.  Source advised that the last time
ANGUILO was confined to Charles Street several years ago they
had a connection through JOE TECCI so that JERRY had his
own meals brought out to to him.  In addition ANGUILO was
also provided "female companionship" to make his stay a little
more comfortable.
```

Exhibit 353-00160

One of Stevie's coups as a rat came in 1980 when he located two Boston killers for easy pickup in Vegas:

```
BS 15-19650
JC/dw
1


          On 11/18/80, BS 955-TE advised that Jimmy Kearns and
Billy Kelly have gone to Las Vegas, Nevada for the week and will
be returning on 11/21/80.  Source advised that it is extremely
doubtful that either one of these individuals will register
with the Las Vegas Sheriff's Office as convicted felons as they
are required to do by law.  Source advised that in view of their
size (Kelly is 6'5", 255 pounds, and Kearns is 6'2", 300 pounds)
they would probably be easy to locate in the casinos.
```

Exhibit 353-00312

And they were.

Once the roundups of hoodlums not connected to Whitey began in the 1980's, those who were under arrest suddenly realized that one get-out-of-jail-free card might be to lead cops to the missing bodies of some gangland victims. That's why Whitey never allowed Pat Nee to know where his victims had been interred; he was

Billy Kelly, now serving life sentence in Florida

concerned that Nee would someday use the bodies against him. But Stevie reported that Pat Nee wasn't the only one interested in the bodies' location:

```
BS 183A-84
JC/mmh
1.


        On October 3, 1985, BS 955-TE advised that SKINNY
KAZONIS called up GEORGE KAUFMAN and said that JERRY ANGIULO
asked him to call and find out if the law ever recovered any
of the BENNETT brothers bodies. KAUFMAN said, "I have no
idea and even if I did, that's a hell of a question to ask me
on a telephone" and hung up on KAZONIS.
```

Exhibit 353-00107

Stevie's strength was the fact that, unlike Whitey, he mixed well among all the city's various criminal and law-enforcement factions. One of his best sources was a corrupt Boston cop named Bill Stuart, who beat a rap on the Bill Bennett murder back in 1969. Stuart, who had been on Wimpy Bennett's payroll, moonlighted as a hitman.

In 1966, he took a contract to murder Elliot Richardson, the future U.S. attorney general who was then running for the same office in Massachusetts. He had been working out at the L Street bathhouse in Southie, which was where Stuart planned to kill him.

"Richardson had a serious drinking problem at the time," Flemmi reported. "Stuart had a hot car and his plan was to run down the inebriated Richardson as he exited the Bathhouse." It was supposed to look like a hit-and-run, and Richardson's

Bill Stuart, Boston detective/hitman

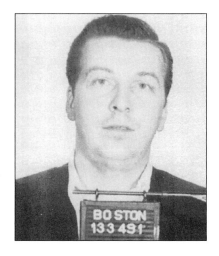

Skinny Kazonis: Had an odd question

blood-alcohol level as shown in the autopsy would make it appear he'd stumbled into the path of the car.

The scheme went awry because so many other Boston cops frequented the Bathhouse, and "Stuart found it difficult to sit in a hot car" while his fellow cops walked by, noticing him.

One of the most interesting tidbits from the FBI rat files came from Flemmi in 1983. The Mafia was in a panic over the recent bugging of the Dog House, Angiulo's headquarters on Prince Street in the North End. They were looking for any scrap of information they could find. Flemmi reported to Connolly that he felt he was being endangered by certain loose lips that might sink his ship:

```
BS 183A-84
JC/sct
1.


          On 8/8/83, BS 955-TE expressed extreme concern for
maintaining the confidentiality of his relationship with
the FBI and stated that there are "leaks" coming from the
United States Attorney's office.  Source advised that he
would not be fearful of Jerry O'Sullivan of the Strike
Force as he trusts him but stated that Jerry Angiulo and
Larry Zannino are being tipped off to details of the
federal investigation on the mafia, i.e., approximate
dates of indictments and number of people to be indicted.
Source advised that the leaks are coming from two sources.
Howie Rubin's girlfriend who works for the U.S. Attorney's
office and Mark Wolf, the Assistant U.S. Attorney.

          Source advised that Wolf is very close to an
unknown Jewish male who is married to the sister of
Bruce Swerling.  Bruce Swerling is the son of the late
Bert Swerling, who was an ex-fire adjuster in Roxbury.
Bert Swerling "did business" on various arsons in
Roxbury with the old Roxbury mob.

          This unknown male who is close to Mark Wolf
is also close to Howie Rubin and everything that Wolf
tells this unknown Jewish male is relayed automatically
to Howie Rubin, who then runs to "Prince Street" to
provide Jerry Angiulo and Larry Zannino with the
information.  In the case of Howie Rubin's girlfriend,
she simply passes on to Rubin any and all information
that she is privy to and this information is in turn
relayed to Prince Street.



          THE ABOVE INFORMATION IS SINGULAR IN NATURE AND SHOULD NOT
          BE DISSEMINATED OUTSIDE THE BUREAU WITHOUT FIRST CONTACT-
          ING THE WRITER.
```

Wolf, of course, was appointed to a federal judgeship by President Ronald W. Reagan. In 1997, he oversaw the hearings that outed both Whitey and Stevie as FBI informants.

Judge Wolf

"Strictly Criminal"

Stevie Flemmi walked to the witness stand, seemingly wearing the same clothes he'd worn the last time he testified in a trial, in Miami, in 2008—a dark green jacket over a lighter green shirt. And that outfit had looked exactly like the one he'd worn in 2004, the first time he testified against Zip Connolly.

It was July 18th, the 24th day of the trial, and the only thing that had changed for Stevie Flemmi was the defendant. Now he was going up against his old partner.

"Good afternoon, sir," said Judge Casper.

"Good afternoon, Judge Casper."

There wasn't much time left in the day's session but the prosecution had wanted to get its star witness onto the stand. He was, after all, not only Whitey's partner in crime, but also his partner in informing—ratting—to the FBI. They had both been "Top Echelon" informants, meeting with the FBI "hundreds of times," almost always together. In fact, Flemmi had been a TE (Top Echelon) informant for the Bureau long before Bulger, recruited even as Whitey was being released from Lewisburg in 1965 after serving nine years for bank robbery.

At age 79, Flemmi was doing life, plus 30 years, in an undisclosed location. He was in what the feds call WITSEC, for cooperating witnesses. It was easier than doing time in general population, although not as easy as defense lawyer Hank Brennan would claim it was in a couple of days.

As questioning began, Flemmi recalled meeting Bulger maybe once in 1969. At the time Flemmi and his then-partner in crime, Cadillac Frank Salemme, were thinking of making a run at the rackets in Southie, as the two Irish factions battled over control

Frank Salemme

of the nickel-and-dime numbers, horse and dog racing, as well as a little loan-sharking.

But that plan never went anywhere—soon Flemmi and Salemme were both on the lam. Whitey and Stevie met up again when Flemmi returned to Boston in 1974, the FBI having conveniently disposed of the murder and car-bombing charges against him. Flemmi immediately became the sixth partner in the recently formed Winter Hill Gang, and he and Whitey developed into a criminal couple of sorts that survived until Whitey fled in December 1994, a few days before Flemmi was arrested.

Fred Wyshak asked him: "What was the nature of your relationship during that 20-year period?"

"Strictly criminal."

This was why the feds had wanted Flemmi on the stand so late in the day. They knew even his incomplete testimony would dominate the next news cycle.

"Was Mr. Bulger an FBI informant?"

"Yes."

"Were you present with Mr. Bulger when he gave information to the FBI?"

"Yes. . . . Over a period of years, over a period of 15, 20 years, numerous, numerous times, hundreds of times."

"Hundreds of times?"

"Yes."

Stevie handled the Mafia information, and Whitey was in charge of dispensing any dirt on "different people from South Boston," mostly his rivals, people like Pat Nee and, most especially, Thomas Nee (no relation).

As time ran out on that first day, Flemmi described the relationship between Whitey and FBI agent Connolly.

"John Connolly would call him on his beeper, and they would converse over the telephone numerous times when I was there. We'd pull over. We were together. We would pull over to the side of the road. Or Connolly would call him or he'd call Connolly at home, or he would call him—whenever John Connolly would call him, he'd return the call."

The next day, Wyshak began by guiding Flemmi through a brief history of his criminal career. After service in the Korean War, Flemmi returned to Boston and quickly fell in with the Bennett brothers, Edward "Wimpy" Bennett and his brother Walter. At the time, Stevie had a bar in Dorchester, and Wimpy was in prison for his role in a scheme involving money from the Brinks robbery of 1950.

"His girlfriend used to come into the bar with her girlfriends, and I was getting kind of friendly with her and she told me who she was, and then when her boyfriend came out, Wimpy Bennett, Ed Bennett had come home, she introduced me to him."

Soon Stevie was in Wimpy's crew, although Stevie never liked the nickname. It was too . . . wimpy. For his own self-esteem, Stevie called Wimpy "the Silver Fox." Bald Fox would have been more like it. The Silver Fox was very self-conscious about his baldness, and was almost never seen in public without a fedora.

Edward "Wimpy" Bennett

In 1961, a gang war broke out in Boston. The Charlestown McLaughlin group was battling with the Somerville mob run by Buddy McLean. Joe Barboza's East Boston gang was with Somerville, and Stevie's younger brother Jimmy "the Bear" was part of that crew.

The situation in the Boston underworld in the 1960's was beyond murky, with all the shifting alliances, the double-crosses and the treachery. During his direct examination, Flemmi detailed a string of ancient murders in which he and everybody was somehow connected to everybody else—"Tommy Timmons was Wimpy Bennett's girlfriend's husband."

In prison, Jimmy Flemmi models a new toupee

Stevie became popular with all the right people—namely, the FBI and In Town. The FBI because he murdered Punchy McLaughlin, a Charlestown killer. Dennis Condon, Rico's FBI partner, was also from Charlestown, and Punchy had been threatening to kill his brother. Even more unforgivable, the G-men had picked up Punchy on a "gypsy" i.e., illegal wire calling Rico and J. Edgar Hoover "a couple of fags."

In September 1965 Rico told Flemmi that Punchy had taken to riding the bus since Stevie had shot his right hand off a month earlier while sitting in a tree as Punchy drove by in a car. One morning when Punchy was dropped off by his girlfriend, Stevie

The Bear's final mugshot, 1979

was waiting at the bus stop. Stevie shot him six times. Before he died, Punchy handed a brown lunch bag to a woman on the bus. It contained a revolver. With only one hand, he couldn't get it out of the bag fast enough to return fire.

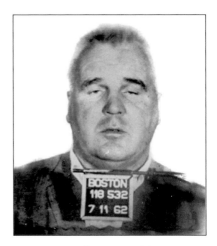
Punchy McLaughlin

In Town—the local Mafia—didn't like Stevie's boss, Wimpy Bennett. He was too tight with Raymond Patriarca, "the Man" in Providence. In Town thought he was the Man's spy in Boston. For some reason, the guys on Winter Hill didn't care much for Wimpy either, perhaps because he and Stevie had blown up Howie Winter's car in 1962 before they switched sides in the gang war.

In January 1967 Stevie shot Wimpy in the head at his Roxbury garage. Three months later his partner Salemme murdered Wimpy's brother Walter. Both bodies were buried on a gun range in Hopkinton. Then Stevie decided he had to kill the third brother, William—"because he was telling people that I was responsible (for his brothers' death)." In December 1967 Billy Bennett was murdered, and Flemmi not only had an IOU from In Town, he also had Wimpy's loan-sharking business.

William Bennett in snow

Stevie was now known as a "capable" guy—he could kill people and get away with it. H. Paul Rico recruited him as a "Top Echelon" FBI informant. From the beginning, his information was always on the money. When he told Rico that Walter Bennett "would not be coming back," Rico knew that Walter Bennett would not be coming back.

In Town asked him if he wanted to be "made." He declined. He left his first wife and moved in with a woman named Marion Hussey, by whom he had three children. In 1969, though, his luck temporarily ran out—he and Frank Salemme were about to be indicted for the murder of William Bennett and for blowing the legs off a lawyer who had been representing Joe Barboza.

The tip about the impending indictments came from, who else, H. Paul Rico. Flemmi and Salemme fled, although Salemme was set up and captured by new FBI agent Zip Connolly in New York in 1972.

Frank Salemme

Stevie ended up in Montreal, keeping up with events in Boston. Spike O'Toole, who had shot his brother Jimmy the Bear during the gang war, asked for forgiveness from Winter Hill. Johnny Martorano called and asked Stevie what should be done with Spike.

"I told him to kill him." And so he did. But then, Johnny owed a favor to Stevie. All those drive-by shootings that wiped out Indian Al's gang in March 1973, they wouldn't have been possible if Stevie hadn't told his friend "Bobby the Greaser" to turn over a special weapon Stevie had left with him, for safekeeping. Martorano had had his eye on it for years.

"I gave him my submachine gun."

Stevie later claimed he didn't even want to leave Montreal in 1974, but that Rico insisted, said he was retiring and might not again have the juice to get the charges dropped. So Stevie returned and joined what was now known as the Winter Hill Gang—the old Somerville crew, plus Whitey Bulger and the consolidated gangs from Southie. Stevie hit it off immediately with Whitey, the only other guy in the leadership from the city of Boston. They had other things in common.

"He didn't drink, he didn't smoke, he worked out regularly."

They were also both rats for the FBI, or soon would be. They trusted each other, so much so that Whitey soon asked Stevie to help him kill Paulie

1971 FBI report

McGonagle, one of the Mullens. The bad blood with McGonagle went back a long way, as this FBI 209 from 1971 indicates. (Whitey is "informant").

The feud started in 1969, when Whitey killed McGonagle's brother Donald, mistaking him for Paul. (A third brother, Robert, was on the Boston Fire Department and was married to Catherine Greig, Whitey's future girlfriend.)

Mr. and Mrs. Robert McGonagle—before she ran off with Whitey

Wyshak then guided Flemmi through the now-familiar Winter Hill murders—Eddie Connors, Tommy King, Richie Castucci.

After murdering the night-club owner for being an informant for the FBI, FBI informant Flemmi drove to the home of Castucci's widow, Sandra, to tell her that her late husband had owed money to the Hill. Eventually she also had to go down to Providence to talk to "the Man," who had likewise put in a bogus claim. She ended up with $8,000 for her husband's fabulously profitable strip club, The Squire.

Richie Castucci in Las Vegas for Sammy Davis Jr.'s wedding

Flemmi and Bulger were beginning to develop the extortions that would prove so lucrative in the 1980's. In 1978, five men were murdered in an after-hours cocaine-and-cash robbery of a Summer Street bar called

Blackfriars. The owner was a guy named Vinnie Solmonte, and he knew a local businessman named Ted Berenson.

"Bulger thought he was ripe for an extortion," Flemmi recalled. "The ingredients were there. He figured that Ted Berenson was doing coke. He had loaned him money. He went to him and said, 'This guy owes some money, you know, to some people, friends of ours, and it has to be paid.'"

WYSHAK: "So who was Ted Berenson?"

FLEMMI: "He was a legitimate real estate developer, a millionaire, but he liked to hang around wiseguys. He was a friend of
Johnny's."

The plan was simple: Zip Connolly was ordered to obtain the crime-scene photographs of the dead bodies from the Boston Police. Whitey showed up at Berenson's office and showed him the photos. Wyshak asked why.

"The guy's a legitimate guy. It frightened him because he was—he was kind of a party guy. He was doing some coke with him. He had loaned some

Extortion victim Ted Berenson, left, outside garage with Whitey and Mafia
hitman Phil "Hole in the Head" Wagenheim

money to Vincent, and he (Whitey) thought that the opportunity was there for him to extort the guy."

So Whitey told Berenson that the dead owner had owed money to hoodlums and that he was going to have to pay them back what Solmonte had borrowed. All BS.

WYSHAK: "And what would happen if he didn't?"

FLEMMI: "He showed him the pictures."

Berenson paid $60,000. It was split, Flemmi said, among himself, Whitey and Johnny Martorano.

WYSHAK: "So why would you extort somebody who's a friend of Martorano's?"

FLEMMI: "That's a good question. It's happened to me quite a few times, a friend of mine."

WYSHAK: "So even if it was somebody who was a friend, you would extort him?"

FLEMMI: "Well, he did to me and my friends."

Wyshak then asked him about the first marijuana dealer to whom they provided "protection," Frank Lepere. At one point Flemmi had to meet with the Mafia to discuss how much Frank Lepere owed a Mafia dealer. Flemmi brought a gun to the meeting.

"I don't trust the Mafia." Again, the present tense. Over the years, Whitey and Stevie collected "well over a million dollars" from Lepere. They even cut Zip in on the money. He got two $25,000 payments at his new home in Thomas Park. Zip was ecstatic.

"He says, 'I'm one of the gang.'"

Then Flemmi was asked who else in the FBI he'd paid off.

"We gave money to Agent Buckley, John Morris, Gianturco, John Newton, John Cloherty—actually, not physically handed the money to John Cloherty, but Cloherty had a problem, a drinking problem during the time the Angiulo wiretapping was going on, and there was a shortage of agents. And he just didn't show up, and they was wondering where he was. So they finally located him, and he had run up a series of checks that were bouncing. So he came to—John Connolly came to Jim Bulger and said to him that he's got a problem, you know, with these checks. He says, can we help him out? So Jim Bulger gave him—I don't know how much the checks come to, but he gave him $2,500 to cover whatever the checks were."

Cloherty would later announce that Billy Bulger was cleared in the 75 State Street scandal, and a few months later, the Senate president would emcee his FBI retirement dinner. Cloherty's sister ended up on the payroll of one of Bulger's loyal Boston senators.

According to Flemmi, Newton got $2,500 on two separate occasions. In return, Newton once gave the boys a case of C-4 plastic explosives, which according to Weeks, Whitey planned to use to blow up the author of this book.

Flemmi said Gianturco and Buckley each received $2,500 at a dinner at the home of Gianturco. Gianturco succeeded Connolly as the director of security at the utility then known as Boston Edison. Gianturco was also the emcee of Zip's FBI retirement dinner, which was videotaped for Whitey Bulger's edification.

At Zip's 2004 racketeering trial in Boston, an FBI secretary recalled going into his desk in those predirect deposit days and seeing 10 or 12 uncashed FBI paychecks. Like Morris before him, Flemmi recalled how Zip was unable to control his spending once he joined the gang.

Gianturco at Zip's 1990 FBI retirement dinner

"He was dressed better than any other agent in the office. That was an indication that on his paycheck, how he was dressing so well. He had a nice car now. Eventually he bought a boat. And when Jim Bulger found out about that, he was upset about it. And he told him he was being too ostentatious, that he had to sell the boat; he's bringing attention to himself and us."

Then Wyshak returned to the subject of Frank Lepere. In 1980, one of Stevie's old partners in an after-hours joint, Sonny Colantonio, was trying to shake Lepere down. Whitey and Stevie decided to kill him.

"We put somebody up to it. We didn't do it ourselves, but I brought it to his attention, and a couple of guys from South Boston took care of it."

WYSHAK: "Who?"

FLEMMI: "It was Tommy Nee, Jimmy Kearns and I believe Pat Linskey was there."

Shortly after this murder, Whitey finally succeeded in getting his sometime-hit-man Tommy Nee arrested, as Zip noted

Early mugshot of Patty Linskey; note the scar on his neck

Thomas Nee
UFAP-MURDER
BS 88-8977

On February 12, 1931, source furnished information regarding the whereabouts of Thomas Nee who was wanted by the Boston, Massachusetts Police Department for several murders. Throughout the years source provided numerous pieces of information regarding Nee and his associates, culminating in the arrest of Nee in New Hampshire. Nee was on the Boston Police Department's "6 Most Wanted Program" for several years.

Source has provided information of a highly sensitive nature, and this information, corroborated where possible, has saved numerous man hours of investigative effort by the Federal Bureau of Investigation.

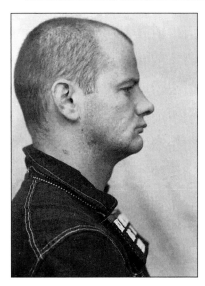

Thomas Nee

Deb Davis

on this report. (Later, when Nee was murdered outside the Pen Tavern, Flemmi said Whitey was greatly relieved.)

Another of the Colantonio murderers, Kearns owed Flemmi; in 1966, as a member of the Barboza gang, he'd been wounded by an In Town hit crew. Flemmi had interceded with Larry Baione to save Kearns' life. Now the chit was called in, and Sonny Colantonio died. And a few months later, a tip from Flemmi to the FBI led to Kearns' arrest in Las Vegas. (See page 167.)

The next subject on the prosecution's agenda was Debbie Davis.

WYSHAK: "Were you in love with her?"

FLEMMI: "Well, I—I loved her, but I wasn't in love with her."

But Whitey didn't like her—"she required a lot of attention. She was a young girl."

One night, Flemmi was attending a birthday party for his girl-friend. Whitey beeped him and told him he had to get somewhere for a meeting with Zip. He told Debbie he had to leave, an argument ensued, and he finally "blurted" out that he had to meet the FBI agent they controlled.

A few months later, her older brother Ronnie—"Gonzo Ronzo"—was stabbed to death in prison. Debbie demanded that Stevie use "his" FBI

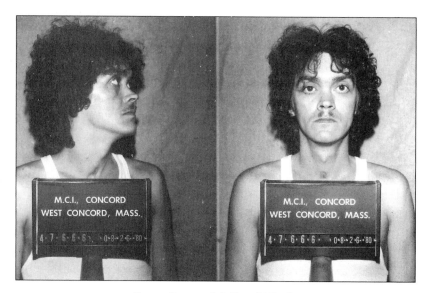

Gonzo Ronzo a/k/a Ronald Davis

agent to find the murderer. Whitey and Zip were not pleased. Then there was the lifestyle issue.

"Well, I bought her a Mercedes. I sent her on vacations. I sent her to Mexico with her mother. I gave her a lot of money. She had a lot of jewelry, and she was—you know people start noticing that."

Finally, according to Flemmi, Bulger decided to kill her. Flemmi argued that Whitey's girlfriend, Catherine Greig, knew about Zip. So did his other girlfriend Teresa Stanley. Zip's wife Marianne had met Whitey. But eventually Whitey wore Flemmi down and he agreed to have her killed. At least that's Stevie's story and he's sticking to it.

"It's affected me," he said, "and it's going to affect me 'til the day I die."

Flemmi said he brought her to the new house he'd just bought for his parents, next to Billy Bulger's. They went into the sun porch and Whitey grabbed her and strangled her. Then he went upstairs and took a nap on an "old rug," because no furniture had been moved in yet. Jack Curran and Pat Nee brought a car around, put the body in it and then drove to Curran's garage. Nee, as always, was then sent home, so he wouldn't know where the body had been buried. After dark, Curran drove Whitey and Stevie to the banks of the Neponset River, handed them a couple of shovels, got the body out of the car, and then drove off.

FLEMMI: "He sat down on the bank, and I dug the hole."

WYSHAK: "Mr. Bulger sat there and watched you? Why doesn't he do any of the work?"

FLEMMI: "That's what he does."

WYSHAK: "What, kill somebody and make everybody else do the work?"

FLEMMI: "Well, he does that."

WYSHAK: "Who was Deborah Hussey?"

FLEMMI: "My girlfriend."

WYSHAK: "Deborah Hussey?"

FLEMMI: "Excuse me. Deborah Hussey was Marion's daughter."

His girlfriend? Was this yet another Freudian slip?

WYSHAK: "Did you have a sexual relationship with her?"

FLEMMI: "Not intercourse, no."

Defense Attorney Hank Brennan

HANK BRENNAN handled the cross-examination. He started with Deb Hussey. He had found a transcript from an old civil deposition in which Stevie had acknowledged holding Deb on his knee when she was a baby. Now he was denying it.

"Is it hard," Brennan asked, "for you to accept the fact that you strangled somebody who sat on your knee as a little girl? Is that hard for you to accept, Mr. Flemmi?"

"I didn't strangle her."

"She would call you 'daddy,' Mr. Flemmi, wouldn't she?"

"Mr. Brennan, I didn't strangle her."

"Mr. Flemmi, did she call you 'daddy?'"

"That's beside the point. The fact of the matter is I didn't strangle her."

Brennan asked Flemmi if he was a good provider. The answer was yes. Then he asked Stevie if he protected the children.

"Well, I think I did on one occasion when she was being held hostage somewhere, I got a phone call, and I went and left the house with a pistol on me and went down and got her released, so I protected her, yes."

Ozzie and Harriet it wasn't. Asked whether he'd had sex with Hussey, Stevie asked Brennan to clarify—"intercourse or what or oral sex? What are you referring to?"

BRENNAN: "When you decided that you were going to have or inflict sex upon her, Mr. Flemmi, did it cross your mind that this is—"

FLEMMI: "Did you say inflict?"

BRENNAN: "Yes, inflict."

FLEMMI: "Consensual."

BRENNAN: "When you decided to have consensual relations with this—"

FLEMMI: "On two occasions, two occasions, let's clarify that, two occasions, and I regret it, a moment of weakness, it happened, but it happened later on in life."

Day 27. Flemmi now knew what he was up against, and he was ready to fight fire with fire. For at least 15 minutes, he took more pounding from Brennan about his sexual relationship with Deb Hussey.

BRENNAN: "You knew that having this relationship with your stepdaughter was wrong, didn't you, Mr. Flemmi?"

FLEMMI: "So didn't Mr. Bulger."

BRENNAN: "I'm asking you—"

FLEMMI: "Yes, yes. But we shared a lot of information, both of us, Jim Bulger and myself. And he had a young girlfriend, 16 years old, that he took to Mexico. That's a violation of the Mann Act. So if you want to come down on me, I just want to relate to you—"

At this point the judge interrupted to tell him to listen to the questions. But Stevie had had enough of that. And his accusation really wasn't anything new—in his DEA-6, his 2003 confession of his life and crimes, he'd even named Whitey's jailbait: Tammy.

Brennan steered the conversation back to the final day of Deb Hussey's life, as Stevie drove his stepdaughter to the death house at 799 East Third Street.

"You didn't tell her you were going to murder her?"

"Of course not."

"You lied to her. Yes?"

"Is that a sensible question?"

Flemmi said he had taken her shopping before they headed over to South Boston.

"You took her shopping," Brennan said, feigning incredulity, "knowing you were going to kill her?"

"That's right, I took her shopping."

"So you thought the last moments of her life would be best spent shopping with you?"

Wyshak objected. Sustained. Eventually Wyshak asked for a sidebar, at which he accused Brennan of trying to "embarrass, humiliate, demean and badger the witness over and over and over again."

Just as his client Whitey Bulger had instructed him to do, no doubt. When Brennan returned to the cross, Flemmi put the murder of Deb Hussey all on his partner.

"Mr. Brennan, he could at any time have prevented that. All he had to do was say 'Pass.' Four words— four little letters, p-a-s-s, that would have been the end of it, and I would have been so happy. He was in control. He was there. He could have walked away."

Brennan mentioned Flemmi's dental pliers—"I couldn't go through with it. I started to and pulled a few teeth out, I tried to anyway."

And then, Brennan said, he dug a hole.

"We dug a hole and buried her, right?" Flemmi corrected him. "We, w-e, we. Kevin Weeks was there."

And then, Brennan pointed out, you dumped her body in an unmarked grave.

"It wouldn't make sense to mark the grave," Flemmi noted.

BRENNAN: "There's a word in jail that's worse than murder, isn't it, and that's pedophile, isn't it, Mr. Flemmi?"

FLEMMI: "I wasn't a pedophile. You want to talk about pedophilia, right over at that table." He pointed right at Whitey.

"No ad-libbing," the judge said. "No adding commentary, just listen to the question and answer it."

Brennan had just begun his questioning on Debra Davis when his partner Carney stood up and asked for a sidebar. He told the judge:

"My client has been writing notes that it is desperate that he be given a bathroom break at this time. It will only be five minutes or less."

What a drag it is getting old.

Once Whitey relieved himself, it was back to business. This time the subject was what Flemmi said once Debra Davis was dead in the basement. His words: "Let her pray!" He didn't dispute that.

"That was how I felt," he said, "that's what I'm saying. That—I blurted it out, 'Let her pray!'"

BRENNAN: "Wasn't it a little late to let her pray?"

FLEMMI: "I was in a semi-traumatic state, I said, 'Let her pray.' I do have a memory of that day, yes, I do, but some of it I don't want to remember, I want to block out because it was such a distasteful act, and it's a guilt trip all these years that I've been on."

Then Brennan accused Flemmi of taking a hammer to smash her teeth after extracting them with his dental pliers. Flemmi was apoplectic.

"I didn't smash her teeth up. Show me where it says that I smashed her teeth up with a hammer. I'd like you to respond to that, please. You accused me of it. You said I smashed her teeth out with a hammer. Show me where I said that. You make that accusation, please respond to it. I didn't smash her teeth out with a hammer."

After Debra's disappearance, Flemmi still hung around the Davis house, saying he would hire a private investigator to find her.

"Mr. Brennan, that's all part of the cover-up."

"You wanted to assure them in the sense that you didn't know where Debbie was, isn't that true?"

"It's all part of the cover-up, yes. When you commit a murder, you cover up on it, you don't admit it to people. I don't know if you're aware of that, you should be, you're an attorney."

Brennan got him to admit that he tapped the phones at Debbie's house. Flemmi said Bulger insisted on it because he'd done the same to his girlfriend Teresa Stanley and had discovered that she was cheating on him.

They got to the bombing of lawyer John Fitzgerald's car in Everett in 1968. It was "ridiculous," Flemmi scoffed. But his partner Salemme asked him to go along with it.

"Why couldn't you say 'no?'" Brennan asked.

"You don't understand the underworld at all, nothing. You're an attorney. You don't know what's going on in the world. I'm giving you the real world."

"That's the real world?"

"That's the real world, right," Flemmi said. "That's the world I was involved in."

Then Brennan asked him why he didn't just start blowing his horn to alert the lawyer. Flemmi shifted in his seat, shaking his head and smiling.

"I'll tell you something, it's hard to answer your questions because—"

The judge interrupted, "Mr. Flemmi, just answer the question." It went on like that, into day 28. Now Brennan was asking about Flemmi's complaints about his stay at MCI-Walpole, and how some "Mafia people" were calling him a "rat."

BRENNAN: "You didn't like that word, 'rat,' did you?"

FLEMMI: "I don't think anybody likes it. I don't think Mr. Bulger likes it."

Flemmi didn't like Walpole either. He wouldn't cut a deal, he wouldn't plead guilty, so they were sweating the Rifleman. It was nothing out of the ordinary, it's how wiseguys like Flemmi get treated if they won't play ball. Brennan asked him about his complaints that he didn't have comfort in visiting his friends and family.

"When you say 'comfort,' I would like to have had a chair."

There was just a partition, Flemmi said, not even a stool.

"I mean, I'm a human being. I would think I would like to have a chair."

The food was horrible too, he said. He lost 35 pounds. As for the sleeping conditions, "I can't sleep anyway, period, even to this day. I couldn't sleep really for years."

Then there was the television situation.

BRENNAN: "You were upset because you didn't have a TV, true?"

"Objection," yelled Wyshak. "It's not the Hilton."

SINCE PLEADING guilty in 2003, Flemmi has been held in what is known as WITSEC, a series of prisons for convicts who have cooperated. It's better than MCI-Walpole, where Flemmi spent those three miserable years, but Brennan tried to make it into a five-star Michelin resort.

"It's like the Club Med of federal facilities," he said.

"You really think so?" Flemmi asked.

"At your prison, when you want to get something to eat, Mr. Flemmi, there's a store that doubles as a delicatessen, isn't there?"

Flemmi leaned forward, tilting his good left ear at Brennan.

"Would you repeat that, please, so I get a real clear understanding of what you're saying?"

"You have a store at your prison that doubles as a delicatessen."

"That," said Flemmi, "is absolutely ridiculous."

"Can you get rib-eye steak?"

"If I gave some of that food to my dog, he'd bite me."

"On Memorial Day and the 4th of July, they celebrate with hamburgers and hot dogs and watermelon, don't they, Mr. Flemmi?"

"You know something? The hot dogs were burnt, the hamburgers were burnt."

Finally, Brennan asked him about being deposed before Zip Connolly's murder trial in Florida. He had been asked then whether he expected to spend the rest of his life in prison, and he replied, "According to the plea agreement, that's the way it looks."

"That's what I said," Flemmi confirmed.

BRENNAN: "And then followed by, 'I don't know.'"

FLEMMI: "I don't know what the future holds."

BRENNAN: "You don't know what your future holds because you're hoping for that opportunity to present itself, Mr. Flemmi?"

FLEMMI: "Everybody hopes at some point in the future something beneficial would happen."

BRENNAN: "I'm not talking about everybody. I'm talking about you. Do you hope, Mr. Flemmi?"

FLEMMI: "I'm still alive, there's always a hope, you never know."

A few minutes later, Flemmi was excused. Still wearing that same green jacket and green shirt, Flemmi was led out of the courtroom by the marshals, to be returned to an unnamed prison where he must spend the rest of his life, plus 30 years.

12

Sole Survivors

It was June 20, 2013, the seventh day of the trial.

"The United States," said prosecutor Brian Kelly, "would call Diane Sussman."

"She may be called," said Judge Denise Casper.

Now that Johnny Martorano had testified about the series of Winter Hill highway machine gunnings that had terrorized Boston in the spring of 1973, it was time to actually hear from a few of the people who had survived the "broadsides," as Martorano called them.

The first witness was Diane Sussman DeTennen, a 63-year-old retired dietician from Los Angeles, married with two children.

Diane Sussman DeTennen outside Federal Court in Boston

In March 1973 she had just turned 23, and was working as an intern at Peter Bent Brigham Hospital. Her boyfriend was Louis Lapiana, a part-time bartender at Mother's, a barroom in the North Station owned by Charlie Raso, who was the partner of Indian Al Angeli.

MILANO ADMIRED his boss, Angeli— "unfortunately," as bookie Charlie Raso put it. Soon, like Indian Al, Milano was growing his hair long, wearing a long coat and finally, and fatally, buying a brown Mercedes like the one his hero owned.

Lapiana was a friend of Milano's. He was working as a bartender that night, and Sussman had been out with her girlfriends at a belated 23rd birth-day party. The plan was that Milano, who had the night off, would return to close the bar, and then give Lapiana and Sussman a ride home to Brighton.

Nobody noticed that there was a

Louie Lapiana

guy standing under the Green Line El with a walkie-talkie. That was John Hurley, a Winter Hill gunman out of Charlestown. He'd been given the job of keeping Mother's under surveillance in case Indian Al showed up. When he saw the brown Mercedes pull up in front, and a guy with long hair and a longer coat get out, he radioed back to Marshall Street. Boilers—stolen cars—were soon on their way to North Station. In the lead car was the Hill's first team—Jimmy Sims driving, Howie Winter and Johnny Martorano with machine guns.

Milano was so proud of his Mercedes. The day before he'd driven it to his brother's, and now he was showing it off to his friends.

"I got the honor of sitting in the front passenger side," Sussman said, "and, you know, getting to play with all the newness of the car."

They drove off toward Brighton, Milano driving, Lapiana in the back-seat. They'd taken three Schlitz beers with them from the bar, and the men were talking about the game of chess they were planning to play when they got back to the apartment.

They were almost home, at the corner of Sparhawk and Market Streets in Brighton, when they pulled up at a red light. To their right was a nunnery.

"All of a sudden there was this noise, a continuous stream of noise of, you know, gunfire, rocks throwing, and it was just nonstop. There was dozens and dozens of whatever. In retrospect, it was a machine gun, but whatever I heard was going on and on. And the car was hit with machine gun bullets."

A California native, Sussman had been taught from childhood to react quickly to anything unusual, and thus possibly dangerous. Specifically, earthquakes. She'd learned certain survival skills.

"I ducked," she said. "Not that you duck in an earthquake, but the minute you hear any rattling or something unusual, there's a procedure, and I think out of training or what, I ducked, because that's probably the only reason I'm here."

When the shooting finally stopped, she climbed up from the floorboard and saw Milano slumped forward over the steering wheel. She asked

Michael Milano's shot-up Mercedes

him if he was okay and got no response. Then she turned around to ask Lapiana how he was, "and his eyes were, like, glazed, and he barely shook his head, and I got a very low noise of 'No.'"

So she leaned over toward Milano and put her hand on the horn. Eventually, she figured, someone would hear it, and come, or at least call the police.

"I remember fighting with the police because they wouldn't let me get in the car or the ambulance with Louis, and I didn't want to be separated from him. I didn't know his status, and I was afraid to leave him."

The nearest hospital, St. Elizabeth's, was only a couple of blocks away. Sussman quickly realized that for some reason she was very hot. She was wearing a pea jacket, and when she took it off, she saw that she was covered with blood. So she just put the jacket back on.

In the emergency room, she discovered she'd been shot in the arm. She spent two days in the hospital. As for her boyfriend, Louis, he was now a quadriplegic, on a respirator. At first, he couldn't even talk. His head was shaved, only the mustache remained of the old Louis.

She had been planning to begin a fellowship in Seattle, and after the police told her that anyone she stayed with in Boston might be in jeopardy themselves, she decided to leave immediately. Back on the West Coast, she communicated with Louis by phone.

"I could talk to Louis. He could not talk back. It was a one-way stream. And the nurses helped out by saying he's smiling or doing something."

After the internship, she went back to Los Angeles, then returned to Boston and got a job at Boston City Hospital.

"By then Louis was doing a little better . . . Louis and I, as close as we were, did a lot of talking, and the rule was, the day I said, 'I need to see Louis' instead of—you know, in my own mind, instead of, 'I want to see Louis' was the time for me to break the relationship, and that happened about two years later."

But, she said, he always remained a part of her life. She returned to southern California, and he was moved to the VA hospital in Long Beach.

"My children grew up from infancy with Louis. Louis' parents were like a second set of grandparents to my children, and I am to this day emotionally connected to Louis. And yes, I was married and my children are not

Louis', but part of the deal was Louis would always be part of my life, and we did things together . . . I was trained to suction him on the respirator, how to handle the wheelchair, what to do if the batteries went low, and, you know— so I developed with him over the years as, you know, over the 28 years."

Louis Lapiana died in 2001.

BRIAN KELLY said, "The United States would call Deborah Scully."

"She may be called," said Judge Denise J. Casper.

Now the prosecution was moving into the story of William O'Brien, who was machine-gunned with another ex-con named Ralph DeMasi on Morrissey Boulevard a few days after the Milano murder in Brighton. This William O'Brien is not to be confused with the William O'Brien who was a member of Whitey's early bank-robbing crew. That William O'Brien was one of the first two criminals (along with Richard Barshard) that Whitey ratted out in 1956 to get a reduction in his sentence. They were the first casualties of Whitey's career as an FBI informant. That William O'Brien was shot to death in 1967 by parties unknown.

This younger William O'Brien was convicted in 1964 of shooting to death yet another O'Brien—George O'Brien—in a barroom brawl in Southie. George O'Brien was 23, and after the trial his mother Mary had handwritten an emotional letter to the Boston newspapers, pleading with them to stop identifying her son as a "victim" of the "gang wars."

Billy O'Brien's first wife was Kay, and they had a daughter, Reba. While O'Brien was serving his manslaughter sentence, Kay had gotten remarried an ex-convict named John Robichaud. He had been shot to death by Winter Hill the previous year.

In 1973, O'Brien's new girlfriend was Deborah Scully, now 61, an employee of the Boston Public Schools. She had grown up in the Old Harbor projects, where the Bulgers lived, and she was able to identify a photograph of a building in the projects with some windows that had shamrocks painted underneath.

"It's the Bulger home," she said. "I used to see him coming in and out of there. Everyone knew that was the Bulger home. It was a very tight-knit community . . . I've had him up to my home, Mr. Bulger."

In March of 1973 William O'Brien—Obie, as she called him—was her boyfriend. She was nine months pregnant with his son.

After dinnertime, she was taking a walk with her daughter, headed toward Old Colony Avenue, when she suddenly saw police cars "flying toward Morrissey Boulevard in every direction, all kinds of police."

When she got back to her mother's apartment, Deborah Scully got the bad news.

"That Obie was dead, that he was machine-gunned out on Morrissey Boulevard."

KELLY: "Were you able to go to William O'Brien's funeral?"

SCULLY: "No."

KELLY: "And why not?"

SCULLY: "I had had his son."

KELLY: "And when was the last time you saw William O'Brien?"

SCULLY: "Two days prior to him dying."

KELLY: "And what did you talk about?"

SCULLY: "The upcoming birth of our child."

Ralph DeMasi outside Federal Court

BRIAN KELLY said, "The United States would call Ralph DeMasi."

"He may be called," said Judge Denise J. Casper.

In March 2013, Ralph DeMasi finished a 21½ year federal bit for an aborted armored car robbery. Before the sentencing of Johnny Martorano in 2004, he had sent a letter to the judge about his brush with death—and the Winter Hill Gang—in 1973.

"I thought someone was taking target practice on the road," DeMasi wrote. "It was my good friend John Martorano."

Whitey was driving that day; he knew Southie and Dorchester better than Jimmy Sims.

In his 2004 letter from prison, DeMasi continued, "I expect to see most people involved in this case in hell someday. I hope you all get there before me. Don't worry, the drinks will be on me."

Now, though, DeMasi wasn't nearly as talkative. He had even brought a lawyer with him, who said his client was "appearing here on an involuntary basis, with a capital 'I' . . . Mr. DeMasi's prior criminal record is such that he has institutionalized anxiety about cooperating with the government on any issue or being perceived to have done so."

In other words, he didn't want to be considered a rat.

The story that had been told about DeMasi was that he was looking to buy guns for the Notarangelis, and that he had reached out to a fellow ex-con, Tommy King, not knowing of King's ties to the gang that was hunting his down.

Now DeMasi had a new explanation for how he happened to get shot on Morrissey Boulevard on March 23, 1973.

PROSECUTOR KELLY: "Do you remember that?"

DEMASI: "No, I don't."

KELLY: "Weren't you part of it?"

DEMASI: "I don't know, tell me about it."

KELLY: "Well, you're the witness, so you're supposed to answer the questions. What happened that day?"

DEMASI: "You want the whole story or just a little bit of it?"

KELLY: "Why don't you start from the beginning?"

DeMasi's new story involved his 1961 Cadillac convertible. It needed some work done on it, so he and his wife drove up from Rhode Island where they were living and dropped it off at the dealership in Boston. Then he drove over to the projects in Southie, apparently in a loaner car, to see the widow Kay Robichaud.

At Kay's apartment, DeMasi said, she told him a story about how she and her 10-year-old daughter by O'Brien were being harassed, and asked DeMasi if he knew anybody who could help them. According to DeMasi, he immediately thought of a Southie guy he'd known in prison, Tommy King.

O'Brien was hanging around his ex-wife's apartment and Kay introduced him to the DeMasis. O'Brien, a stevedore by trade, wanted to get a cake for his daughter's birthday the next day, but he didn't have a car. So, DeMasi claimed, he suggested they use his loaner to visit some of the barrooms and clubs King frequented and try to find him. O'Brien drove, and they stopped by several ginmills, never finding King but leaving Robichaud's number for him to call.

Finally King called back, and suggested they meet at Linda Mae's, on Morrissey Boulevard. That was fine with O'Brien, because he could get a birthday cake there. O'Brien drove DeMasi down and while DeMasi and King talked, O'Brien bought his daughter's birthday cake.

"He had nothing to do with the conversation with Tommy. So, we all broke up, left, and Billy's driving, and it was dark. So I looked back just before I got in the car. I looked back to see where Tommy went. He got in a car with three other guys, but I don't know who they were."

They were Whitey Bulger, Howie Winter and Johnny Martorano.

O'Brien and DeMasi pulled out onto Morrissey Boulevard, heading north back toward Southie.

"I said Billy, keep your eye on the rearview mirror, the side mirror. If a car comes up fast, hit the gas. He started laughing, ah Ralph you're—ain't nobody going to hurt us, blah, blah, blah. I said Billy, pay attention, I got bad vibrations. Watch your mirrors, if a car comes up fast, hit the gas. He keeps laughing. All of a sudden, a car pulls up, people start shooting at us. When it was over, Billy O'Brien was dead, I had eight bullets in me."

As the firing started, O'Brien floored the car and yelled "What the fuck!" Those were his last words. The car fishtailed, hit the guardrail and came to an abrupt stop.

"He must have died instantly. As soon as he said 'What the fuck!' we started fishtailing."

According to the medical examiner, O'Brien suffered 20 gunshot wounds.

"What did I do? I got hit and I got thrown forward, and just instinct made me go down as low as I could near the floorboards . . . My adrenaline was going. I didn't have a gun, but I had a stiletto. Pulled the stiletto out, opened the door, jumped out of the car. The cars that were shooting at us stopped about 30 yards up ahead. The two shooters were getting out. I ran toward them, hoping that I could stab one of them and get a gun from him. All right? When they saw me coming, one of them yelled, 'Here he comes!' and they jumped back in the car and burned rubber. My adrenaline is going. I start running after him—"

William O'Brien dead in his car

O'Brien's vehicle after the shooting

It was at this point that Kelly interrupted.

"Now wait a minute," he said. "You were shot eight times and you were running at guys with a knife?"

"Right," DeMasi said. "I got shot here, my shoulder, and my back a number of times."

KELLY: "I take it, given your presence here today, you survived that shooting?"

DEMASI: "It's pretty obvious, ain't it?"

Kelly tried to ask another question, but DeMasi said he'd finish the story.

"So after I realize I'm a nitwit running after a car that's burning rubber, I stop. When I stop, my whole side was paralyzed. I walked back to the car. I'm looking in. I yell, Billy, Billy. Looked in, got close because it was dark. The whole side of his face was blood. It's obvious he was dead."

Delirious, DeMasi started walking down Morrissey Boulevard. An MDC police car pulled up.

"A cop jumped out. 'Holy shit! You're all blood all over!' Yeah. I said, 'Yeah, what happened?' He said, 'You got shot.' I said, 'What did you shoot me for?' I was disoriented a little bit. He said, 'I didn't shoot you. Get in the car.' 'No, I ain't getting in the car. So you can shoot me again?' He goes, 'Come on, get in the car.' He grabbed me, put me in the car, took me to the hospital."

Three days later, DeMasi checked himself out of the hospital to go to O'Brien's funeral. When the cops spotted him, they arrested him. The charge: getting shot. It was a violation of his parole.

On cross-examination, Carney asked him what had happened to him after he got out of prison March 1.

"Did the government give you $20,000 to help you resettle your life?"

"No," said DeMasi. "They gave $16, I think about 10 of it was mine."

IT WAS June 21, 2013, the eighth day of the trial.

Prosecutor Zach Hafer said, "Your Honor, the government calls Frank Capizzi."

"He may be called," the judge said.

Another sole survivor—of the March 18, 1973 machine-gunning on Commercial Street. Two other passengers survived—Al Angeli and Hugh "Sonny" Shields. But Angeli was murdered a year later, and Shields has since passed away.

So Frank Capizzi, age 78, was subpoenaed to testify—another extremely reluctant witness. Even before the Commercial Street shooting, he had already survived two assassination attempts, both of which he blamed on Whitey. (In one of the shootings, a witness described the gunman as "not a kid." Whitey was 43 at the time.) Capizzi now lived in Arizona, but he was born

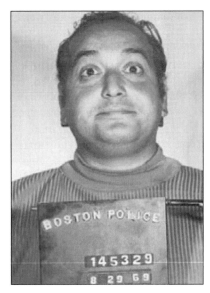

Frank Capizzi

in Boston, graduated from Boston English High School in 1953, went into the Coast Guard and later "managed an infamous spot called The Looking Glass."

In the late 1960's he got involved with Al Angeli—Indian Al. They owned a ski lodge in Vermont that burnt down under mysterious circumstances. As for the shooting, he too told a story different from the earlier versions. In his current version, Angeli was not in the car. The passengers were himself, Shields and a 48-year-old World War II vet named Al "Bud" Plummer. When they got into a car near the Aquarium, they were planning to drop Capizzi off to visit his grandmother in the North End.

Hafer asked him to explain what happened as they drove north on Commercial Street.

"A firing squad hit us."

HAFER: "Would you describe that?"

Capizzi paused for a moment, long enough so that everyone would notice how long he was not speaking. Finally he spoke again.

"Multiply that by about a hundred, and for that many seconds, which is maybe 2½ minutes, for 2½ minutes, about a hundred slugs hit the automobile, and it imploded."

He was sitting in the backseat behind the driver, Plummer, which saved his life. Finally the shooting stopped.

"Unbelievably, although I had been hit in the head and could feel warm blood running down my neck and excruciating pain in my back, I said, 'Let's get the fuck out of this car. Bud, come on.' And I put my hand up, and my hand went into his neck where his head should have been."

According to the medical examiner, Plummer suffered "a number of gunshot wounds." He was killed by the bullets that "transected the great blood vessels, being the carotid arteries and the jugular veins on both sides of the neck."

Somehow, Capizzi got back to Winthrop and checked into the hospital there, where he was operated on.

"And the doctors told my wife, although the operation lasted four hours, that it would be better to leave the 18 or 20 or 16 pieces in my back. They took out what they could, which was about 11 slugs."

Capizzi, his wife and two children immediately hit the road. Like De-Masi, he wrote a letter to the judge who sentenced Martorano, saying that as he fled west, his children "had the job of cleaning festering wounds and picking up bits of lead from my back as they surfaced."

In the letter, Capizzi said he briefly returned to Boston a few years later. He then received a visit, from BPD Detective Eddie Walsh and FBI agents Dennis Condon and Zip Connolly.

"I looked into John Connolly's Machiavellian eyes and told (him), Mr. Connolly, James Bulger shot me three times!!! . . . . Dennis Condon listened attentively, writing it all down."

No arrests were ever made, and Capizzi fled Boston again.

"If I may," he explained, "my wife and children were living in the throat of the dragon for 40 years without any help from anyone."

On cross-examination, Carney asked him about the gangs of Boston in the early 1970's.

CARNEY: "One of them, one of the criminal gangs, was headed by
    Gennaro Angiulo in the North End of Boston?"
CAPIZZI: "That's what the papers say."
CARNEY: "Did you know that yourself?"

CAPIZZI: "You know, ask me a more specific question. Did I know that? The question would be, Who didn't know that?"

Then Carney moved on to Al Angeli.

CARNEY: "How did Al make his living?"

CAPIZZI: "Ask Al."

CARNEY: "I'd like to ask you, sir."

CAPIZZI: "You will."

CARNEY: "How did Al make his living?"

CAPIZZI: "How Al made his living. I would say he was as corrupt as the rest of them."

When Carney asked Capizzi if he made his living as an illegal gambler, Capizzi said, "I'm going to invoke my right against—against—"

The judge had already signed an immunity order for him, so she called him over to the sidebar to explain what that meant. It didn't seem to sink in at first.

"Your Honor," Capizzi began, "I had a Code Blue, a cardiac arrest. Besides encephalitis meningitis, I was in a coma for three weeks."

"I'm sorry to hear that," said the judge.

She then again explained that since she had signed the immunity order, he would have to answer the questions, and his statements, if they were truthful, could not be used against him.

"You mean," he said, "I don't have a right to invoke my right?"

He still didn't seem to quite get it, so the judge said she would send for an attorney that he could talk to.

"Your Honor," Capizzi said, "can I have the comment in my record that I was in the coma and that I was in cardiac arrest in case something happens to me here?"

"Well sir," said Judge Casper, "it's reflected on the record, as is everything else."

"And that I was in a coma for several weeks. . . ."

At the defense table, Whitey Bulger continued doodling aimlessly on his legal pad, never even looking up.

Will He or Won't He?

By the end of the prosecution's case, there was really one question left: Would Whitey Bulger take the stand in his own defense?

The prosecution had proven its case beyond a reasonable doubt, and then some. Carney had conceded as much, from the opening. The only mystery now was, would Whitey go out in a blaze, not so much a blaze of glory, but at least a small flame of bluster, with perhaps a flicker of rationalization thrown in?

Most courtroom observers figured no way. Anthony Cardinale, the defense lawyer who'd been representing Frank Salemme in 1997 when the FBI finally admitted that Whitey and Stevie were informants, was in the courthouse taking bets against Whitey testifying with anyone who was interested in getting some action.

For one thing, the Cardinale theory went, Whitey's still-outsized ego wouldn't permit a bruising cross-examination. He'd already lost his composure with both John Morris and Kevin Weeks, and the prosecutors had been waiting for this moment for 20 years—they were champing at the bit to have a go at him. Cross-examination wouldn't be good for his brother Billy either. The feds had shown the former Senate president absolutely no deference thus far, and this would be a perfect opportunity to put everything they had uncovered about him and his decades of wheeling and dealing on the table.

And it would all be on the record. Everything.

Still, Carney continued to hint, off the record, that anything was still possible, that no final decisions had been made, etc. The judge took to asking him about Whitey at least once a day, usually more.

Carney would give her his customary non-committal answer, and she'd shake her head sadly, and tell him she'd be asking him the same question again tomorrow, and then Carney would shake his head sadly, and tell her he'd be giving her the same answer tomorrow . . .

Pat Nee

Whitey had badly wanted to put his old partner-in-crime Pat Nee on the stand—"classic rat behavior," Cardinale had sneered—but Nee didn't even make it to the courtroom before he was excused on Fifth Amendment grounds. Another key defense witness was to be Marion Hussey, Deb's mother and Stevie's common-law wife. But she was apparently too ill to testify, and Carney had to settle for reading her testimony from some long-forgotten deposition.

Nunzio Orlando, a state trooper who had once accused Johnny Martorano's cop handlers of letting him drift back into the rackets, was also scrubbed. Carney, already playing a very weak hand, now drew . . . a joker.

Bob Fitzpatrick

IT WAS July 29, 2013, the 31st day of the trial.

"Your Honor," said Hank Brennan, "the defense calls Robert Fitzpatrick."

On paper, he seemed like he would make a decent witness. Briefly, in the early 1980's, he'd been the acting special agent in charge of the Boston office. He'd met Whitey. His reputation as a Whitey authority, such as it was, was made shortly before the murder of Brian Halloran. He'd told then U.S. attorney (and future governor) William Weld that "I wouldn't want to be standing next to that guy."

A few days later, Halloran was shot to death on Northern Avenue.

He'd parlayed that offhand remark into a book contract and numerous TV appearances. But apparently Carney and Brennan hadn't done their homework, because on direct they let him go on and on about his remarkable career in the Bureau, from his finding of the rifle that killed Martin Luther King, Jr. to the arrest of Gennaro Angiulo. After some desultory inside-baseball testimony by Fitzpatrick about the Boston FBI office, prosecutor Brian Kelly got up and began his cross-examination.

KELLY: "Sir, it's fair to say, isn't it, you're a man who likes to make up stories?"

FITZPATRICK: "I beg your pardon."

KELLY: "You're a man who likes to make up stories, aren't you?"

FITZPATRICK: "No."

KELLY: "In fact, for years you've been trying to take credit for things you didn't do, isn't that right?"

FITZPATRICK: "No."

KELLY: "Well, in fact, at the beginning of your testimony, didn't you gratuitously claim credit for arresting the mob boss, Jerry Angiulo?"

FITZPATRICK: "I wish I did arrest the—I did arrest him."

KELLY: "Not what you wished you did, didn't you tell this jury, 'I also arrested Angiulo.'"

FITZPATRICK: "I did arrest Angiulo."

KELLY: "That's a total bald-face lie, isn't it?"

And then Kelly proved that that's exactly what it was. The prosecutor showed him the 302 report of the arrest; Fitzpatrick's name was nowhere to be seen. Kelly read Fitzpatrick a passage of purple prose from his book about how he "hustled" Angiulo out of Francesco's Restaurant after telling the underboss he wouldn't cuff him until they were outside.

> KELLY: "Never happened, did it?"
>
> FITZPATRICK: "What never happened?"
>
> KELLY: "You didn't cuff him outside the restaurant?"
>
> FITZPATRICK: "'We,' this is 'we cuffed him.' I never claimed that I cuffed him. It says, 'we.'"
>
> KELLY: "'Before he could react, I hustled him from the table.'" You told him that you would not cuff him until 'we were outside.'"
>
> FITZPATRICK: "Oh yeah, I did say that."

The main thrust of Fitzpatrick's direct testimony had been that Bulger was not really an informant because what he provided was little more than worthless gossip. Kelly picked up Fitzpatrick's book again.

> KELLY: "In this book, you refer to Bulger as an informant over 100 times, don't you?"
>
> FITZPATRICK: "I'm not saying that that's me exactly saying that, I'm reporting what other people said."
>
> KELLY: "Well, how about on page 29: 'SAC Sarhatt briefed me on the informant'"? . . . There's no question in your mind that the FBI had Mr. Bulger as an informant, is there?"
>
> FITZPATRICK: "He was an informant. I went out to interview him as an informant."

Kelly was just warming up. Fitzpatrick, it would soon become clear, was forced out of the FBI after 22 years, three years short of his pension. Kelly apparently had Fitzpatrick's entire FBI personnel file in front of him. He showed Fitzpatrick a letter about the demotion he first received.

"This letter," Fitzpatrick said, "was sent before the settlement agreement, which expressly stated that this letter was never to be read again."

Then Kelly brought up another of Fitzpatrick's boasts—that he had found the rifle used to shoot Dr. Martin Luther King, Jr. in Memphis in 1968. Kelly showed him the official 200-page FBI report on the murder of King and asked ungrammatically but forcefully, "Where is you?"

Next he moved on to the murder of John McIntyre.

> KELLY: "Don't you put a phony dialogue between James Bulger and John McIntyre in your book?"
>
> FITZPATRICK: "It's probably part of the research."
>
> KELLY: "It's probably completely made up, isn't it?"
>
> FITZPATRICK: "It's part of the research."
>
> KELLY: "What research substantiated your claim that Bulger said to McIntyre, 'God's not here, I'm here, do you believe in God, Johnny? Do you go to church, what's God done for you anywhere compared to all I've done, and this is how you pay me back.' By fucking me in the ass? That's completely made up, isn't it?"

Fitzpatrick noted that he had a co-author.

IT WOULD hardly have seemed possible, but the next morning it got even worse for Fitzpatrick, as Kelly began asking him about his testimony the previous day. He said he couldn't remember.

> KELLY: "You don't remember yesterday's testimony?"
>
> FITZPATRICK: "No, I don't."
>
> KELLY: "You don't recall your testimony from yesterday?"
>
> FITZPATRICK: "You're asking me to recall something that I may not recall."
>
> KELLY: "I'm asking you, first of all, to recall something you said yesterday and you don't recall."

FITZPATRICK: "Fine. I just don't recall."

KELLY: "Are you on medication or anything?"

FITZPATRICK: "I am on medication, yes."

KELLY: "Does it affect your memory?"

FITZPATRICK: "I don't believe so, but I'm on medication."

KELLY: "Do you have any medical issues with your memory?"

FITZPATRICK: "Not that I recall."

KELLY ALSO delved into a little-known part of Zip Connolly's career—his master's degree from Harvard. In 1981, Fitzpatrick wrote Connolly a "glowing recommendation," as Kelly put it, to Harvard.

A few months later, while Connolly was studying for his master's degree in public administration at Harvard, he tipped Whitey Bulger to the fact that Brian Halloran was talking to the FBI. A few weeks later Halloran and Michael Donahue were shot to death by Whitey.

Kelly read to Fitzpatrick from his book: "I knew full well that Halloran was killed because Connolly had told Bulger he was talking, making him a direct accessory to murder, as the Wolf hearings revealed 16 years later."

Kelly looked up from the book and spoke to Fitzpatrick: "In fact, sir, after the Halloran and Donahue murders in May of '82, you didn't call up Harvard and tell them that John Connolly might not be Harvard material after all, did you?"

"I don't recall that," Fitzpatrick admitted.

Then Kelly picked up another document. It was Zip's evaluation from 1982, when he was leaking—and Fitzpatrick according to his own book knew he was leaking—information to serial killers that had led to at least two murders.

KELLY: "And didn't the evaluation refer to Mr. Connolly and say, 'His performance has been at the level to which all should aspire to attain but few will realistically reach.' Those were your words, weren't they, sir?"

FITZPATRICK: "Not exactly."

By the time Fitzpatrick finally limped off the stand, the odds in the court-room on Whitey testifying were off the board. No way could he withstand that kind of beating.

THAT WAS Tuesday, July 30. Carney and Brennan went through the motions for a couple of more days, bringing in a handful of witnesses who added next to nothing to the record. By Friday, they could stall no longer.

Carney stood up and made the announcement. His client would not be testifying. A low sigh of disappointment, if not in the courtroom, then at least in the "overflow rooms" where the press and public were watching the trial on closed-circuit televisions.

Whitey rose from his chair as Judge Denise Casper addressed him directly:

"You understand that this is the juncture of the case at which I ask for a decision about whether or not you're going to testify. Mr. Carney has just represented on your behalf that you're not going to testify."

"Correct," said Whitey.

"And you have done so after careful consideration, sir?"

"Yes, I have," said Whitey.

"Have you done it after consultation with your attorney?"

"Yes."

"And are you making this choice voluntarily and freely?"

"I'm making the choice involuntarily because I don't feel—I feel that I've been choked off from having an opportunity to give an adequate defense and explain about my conversation and agreement with Jeremiah O'Sullivan. For my protection of his life, in return, he promised to give me immunity."

"Choked off"—another Freudian slip?

But this was what Whitey couldn't say on the stand, because the prosecution would have eviscerated him. O'Sullivan was dead, before his death had denied making any such agreement, couldn't have offered any such immunity deal under any circumstances anyway—it was all just another Winter Hill blame-it-on-the-dead-guy lie. After all the years, and all the crimes, Whitey was still in South Boston, even if it was a courtroom. And South Boston was where he did his best lying, whether it was about Tommy King going off to Canada to rob banks, or getting a contract to kill Ray

Slinger and Jack Cherry, or being owed money by John Callahan, or having counterfeit bills for Paulie McGonagle . . .

The judge nodded. She'd played it straight all the way, and at this late date she didn't want to leave behind the slightest grounds for the inevitable appeal.

"I understand your position, sir," she said, "and certainly you're aware that I have considered that legal argument and made a ruling."

"I understand," Whitey said.

"I understand, sir, if you disagree with it, okay?"

"I do disagree," Whitey said, "and that's the way it is. And thing is, as far as I'm concerned, I didn't get a fair trial, and this is a sham, and do what youse want with me. That's it. That's my final word."

From the gallery, Michael Donahue's widow Patricia yelled: "You're a coward." (A few minutes later, outside the courthouse, her son Tommy would step it up a notch, describing his father's killer as "a rat coward.")

After shouting, "Silence!" the judge returned to her script. Pro forma, Judge Casper asked Whitey one final time if he'd decided not to testify.

"Correct," he said, and sat down. He didn't seem to realize, "they" already had done to him what they wanted—they had destroyed the only thing that still mattered to him, his legend.

Case 1:99-cr-10371-DJC Document 1254-13 Filed 07/31/13 Page 1 of 1

1395

Whitey, buff as always, on vacation from the rackets

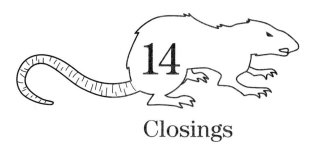

Closings

It was August 5, 2013, the 36th day of the trial.

"I will ask Mr. Wyshak," said Judge Casper, "to begin the government's closing."

The testimony was over. With the jury's inevitable guilty verdict looming, the lawyers representing the government and the defendant each had three hours to make their final pitches to the jury.

For the prosecution, the unenviable task was to somehow compress 20 years of horrific evidence into 180 minutes.

Conversely, Jay Carney and Hank Brennan had to somehow stretch one simple argument—jury nullification, that is, punishing the government for its misdeeds by acquitting their monstrous client—over three long hours.

Carney and Brennan had decided on a somewhat unusual technique, splitting the closing. Brennan, the junior partner, would lead off, dealing more with the abstract issue of governmental misconduct, while Carney would handle the specific attacks on the three main government witnesses, Martorano, Flemmi and Weeks.

But first up was prosecutor Fred Wyshak, with an argument he'd been polishing and delivering in his mind for the better part of two decades.

He began with a counter to the defense's coming attacks on the main witnesses.

"The government did not choose these men," he said. "The reason these men are here testifying before you in this courtroom is because of the choices that James Bulger made in his life. For everything you want to say about them, he's the same."

The issues, he told them, are not FBI corruption, or incompetence, or overly lenient sentences.

"Don't get distracted by the defense arguments about irrelevant issues that are designed to keep you from focusing on what's important for you to decide the evidence in this case."

No system, he said, is perfect.

Then he brought up Carney's puzzling opening seven weeks earlier, in which the lawyer had conceded many of the crimes that Whitey was indicted for.

"He told you that his client, James Bulger, was involved in illegal gambling, loan-sharking, drug dealing, extortion. We don't dispute that, we

Senate President Bulger congratulates Zip on his retirement from FBI, 1990.
Whitey was given a videotape of the dinner

agree with that. The evidence has proven it. He told you that James Bulger made millions of dollars from engaging in this criminal activity. Again, we agree. The evidence has shown that as well."

Throughout the course of the trial, the prosecutors had mentioned William M. Bulger's name almost as often as the defense had brought up the name of Patrick Nee, the Mullen who got away. Now Wyshak got in the first of several final shots against Whitey's little brother.

"John Connolly cared more about his relationship with James Bulger and William Bulger than he did about doing his job. He saw a way not only to enhance his career, but also to protect Mr. Bulger."

Which Mr. Bulger, he did not specify.

Then he briefly outlined the recent history of organized crime in Boston, and how the Winter Hill Gang prevailed in the gang wars of the 1960's in which more than 60 men were slain.

"These men were the victors, these men were the survivors. They were armed to the teeth. They were organized, they were feared. They operated like a paramilitary organization . . . They hunted their targets. These men didn't hunt animals, ladies and gentlemen, they hunted people. That's why they are so successful. These men were the scariest people walking the streets of Boston."

Now Wyshak circled back again to the man who had never once ventured into Courtroom 11, the 79-year-old younger brother of Whitey, William M. Bulger, with his $200,000-a-year state pension.

"There's another factor that we can't ignore in this case, and that's Mr. Bulger's brother, William, who was one of the most powerful politicians in Massachusetts at the time . . . It was John Connolly's dream to become Police Commissioner of the Boston Police Department. Who was going to get him there? William Bulger. That's another reason why John Connolly aligned himself with James Bulger. Not only did it enhance his personal career, it cemented his relationship with William Bulger for that next job as Police Commissioner of the city of Boston."

Wyshak knew he couldn't say enough about John Martorano and his 20 murders. He took to repeating himself. What were Martorano's crimes? "Horrific, horrific." Did he deserve to spend the rest of his life in prison? "Absolutely, absolutely."

But, he said, there had been no evidence against him in any of the murders he'd confessed to. Actually, had Martorano been tried it would most likely have come down to Stevie Flemmi testifying against Martorano, instead of vice versa. But Flemmi's word by itself would have been worthless, because he had already been convicted of perjury, although that fact was not something Wyshak wanted to muddy the waters with at this final stage of the trial.

The alternative to not cutting deals with murderers, Wyshak suggested, was leaving it up to the Boston FBI office to end the crime wave. And at the time the Boston office was being run by the likes of Bob Fitzpatrick, who not so coincidentally had been the defense's first witness a few days earlier.

"Bob Fitzpatrick I think is a poster boy for what was wrong in the Boston FBI at the time. This is a man who resigned in disgrace from the FBI. Every piece of evidence that's before you in this trial is inconsistent with his claim that he was sent to Boston to clean up the Boston office. When it suits him, he solved every crime since Jack the Ripper."

Yet, Wyshak continued, while Fitzpatrick was the interim head of the Boston FBI office, Whitey and his crew murdered seven people—"and Bob Fitzpatrick wants to tell you he couldn't do anything about it."

So the prosecutors had to cut a deal with Martorano. Wyshak repeated the words, "Horrific, horrific."

Next Wyshak began outlining the 19 murders. By the time he reached Paulie McGonagle, he was giving the jury the exhibit numbers where they could read the old FBI reports about how as far back as 1971, Whitey was complaining that McGonagle, another of the Mullens, was hunting him.

"Mr. Bulger is not the kind to forgive and forget," Wyshak said. Then he recalled Flemmi's testimony how he and Whitey used to walk on Tenean Beach in Dorchester, where Whitey had buried McGonagle below the high-tide water line. Whitey would always say, "Drink up, Paulie. Drink up, Paulie."

"That's the level of humanity that the defendant in this case is operating at."

Whitey's expressed fear of McGonagle, Wyshak said—"that's Exhibit 359-A, No. 35600392. So if you're interested in looking at that document, that's where you can find it."

And just to make it easier for the jury, Wyshak put the report up on the courtroom screen.

Then he pointed out Whitey's reminiscence about the murder of Eddie Connors, as recorded in the fall of 2012 at the Plymouth County Correctional Facility, when he twice mimicked a machine gun: "Rat-a-tat-tat."

"That tape is in evidence, Exhibit 663, if you want to listen to it again."

Next he put up Exhibits 535 and 537—photographs of the skull of yet another Mullen, Tommy King, with the fatal bullet hole visible.

"And, again, Bulger, what does he tell Margaret King, the wife of Thomas King? He tells her this story about, well, he went up to Canada to rob banks, and he's not going to be around for a while. Now, if he has nothing to do with this murder, why is he making up a story for Margaret King?"

Wyshak then briefly recounted the story of how, after murdering King and burying him under the Neponset River bridge, Whitey had murdered still another Mullen, Buddy Leonard, left his corpse in King's car and then dictated an FBI report to Connolly about how King has been ordered never to return to Boston.

"Exhibit 359-B, No. 35600378," Wyshak told the jury.

Then Wyshak directly confronted the Pat Nee conundrum. He knew Carney was going to bring it up; Whitey would have insisted upon it. The man who claimed he was not a rat could not abide having Nee still

> On 11/21/75, source advised that TOMMY KING who recently murdered FRANCIS X. "BUDDY" LEONARD, was told by the MULLIN gang that he is to remain out of the Boston area on a permanent basis. According to source, KING was forced to accept the decision but agreed that it would be best if he never came back in light of speculation that the police are believed to have a couple of witnesses to the LEONARD murder. Both the MULLIN gang and the Winter Hill people made the decision and according to the source they plan to support KING while he is away.

> On 11/10/75, source advised that BUDDY LEONARD's death was the result of a violent argument between himself and TOMMY KING. Source stated that to his knowledge, the murder was not a sanctioned "hit" but rather grew out of some "bad blood" between the two. Source speculated that KING would probably face some reprimand from the MULLIN gang for killing LEONARD in that manner although it would probably not be anything severe as LEONARD was disliked by almost all of the MULLIN crew, and himself had been responsible for a few murders.

King–Mullen documents

a free man after allegedly committing at least two murders with him. Not only that, but now, at age 68, Nee was starring in a new "reality" TV series on the Discovery Channel, *Saint Hoods*. It had to be driving Whitey crazy.

His lawyers had returned to the question of Pat Nee's crimes over and over, so Wyshak brought up Kevin Weeks' testimony about the man in the ski mask who had been in the backseat of "the tow truck," the gang's hit car, when Halloran and Donahue were slaughtered.

"The next morning they meet at Carson Beach with Pat Nee, and what does Pat Nee say? Sure enough, 'My gun jammed.' So that man in the backseat with the ski mask I submit to you is Pat Nee."

So now it would be up to Suffolk County district attorney Dan Conley to decide whether to indict the Discovery Channel's newest star for the two homicides.

The evidence against Whitey hadn't just come from the three killers, Wyshak continued. Brian Halloran's brother, Barry, a former state trooper, had talked with his brother about the murder contract the gang had offered him on World Jai Alai owner Roger Wheeler.

"But he turned it down. And why did he say? He said he didn't want to wind up like Tommy King, the guy that they lured down to Carson Beach . . . He thought that this was another scam to lure him to his death, and he didn't go for it. Again, a tidbit of evidence but something that gives the ring of truth to all the other evidence in the case."

Next Wyshak put up on the courtroom screen Exhibit 282, one of Zip Connolly's 209s from July 7, 1982.

"Callahan was close to a Cuban group who he was impressed with as being very bad. Source added that lately Callahan's relationship with this group has cooled, and Callahan is supposed to be avoiding them."

Wyshak paused to let that sink in.

"Now either John Connolly has a crystal ball, or he's in league with Bulger and Flemmi to murder John Callahan. How does he know three weeks before the fact that Callahan is going to be murdered in Florida and that Callahan's belongings are going to be found in the Cuban section?"

Then he put up Exhibit 318. It's from Zip Connolly, "and if you recall, it's an alibi, an alibi for James Bulger, not only for the Wheeler murder but for the Callahan murder, (dated) April 7, 1983. Now, what is an FBI agent doing providing an alibi for the head of an organized-crime group regarding two murders?

"Again, this document says it all about the nature of this relationship."

At this point, more than 2½ hours into his closing, Wyshak felt entitled to engage in a little armchair psychoanalysis of his longtime nemesis.

"He's the actor. He's the Type A personality in this group. He's always the one there with the gun pulling the trigger. But what does he do after that, the case in (Bucky) Barrett, the case in (Deb) Davis, the case in (John) McIntyre. He goes and takes a nap. And he did the same thing after he murdered Deborah Hussey."

He recalled bookie Dick O'Brien's story about the runaway bookie who wanted to go into another business. And how Whitey told him his crew had another business too: "We kill assholes like you."

WYSHAK: "And Mr. Bulger, if you remember, thought that was very humorous."

After three hours and 15 minutes, Wyshak finished with a legal point—consciousness of guilt. In her instructions to the jury the next day, the judge would tell the jury that they could use evidence of flight in determining Whitey's guilt.

"The defendant ran away," Wyshak said. "But this is more than a man who ran away. If you take a look at the cash on this table, this is a man who lived in an apartment with holes cut in the wall, holes in the wall that held $822,000 in cash, holes cut in the wall that held more than 30 weapons, most of which contained bullets, most of which were loaded. This is a man who had identifications for half a dozen different people. Clearly this is a man who was hiding. This is a man who knew he was under indictment. This is a man who had a guilty conscience."

Did he? You wouldn't know it to look at Whitey, doodling on his legal pad.

HANK BRENNAN, a former state prosecutor, went first for the defense. He started with Wyshak's description of "the Hill" as some of the most dangerous murderers ever to walk the streets of Boston.

Memorandum

To : SAC, BOSTON (137A-4075)   Date 4/7/83

From : SA John Connolly, Jr.

Subject : BS 1544-TE

     The following is being submitted at the request of the C-2 Supervisor:

     With regard to the murder of Roger Wheeler, I specifically recall watching a national news program on one of the major networks during the 7:00 p.m. time slot on which program they had coverage of the Wheeler murder. My recollection is that the murder had taken place some time that day and I believe there may have been some brief film footage regarding the murder.

     Following my watching the news program I placed a telephone call to captioned source in order to set up a contact. I discussed the news item regarding the Wheeler murder which source had also watched. Source commented that it was probably a couple of guys trying to kidnap Wheeler for a ransom and he fought them off. We had no further discussion that I can recall regarding the Wheeler murder.

     With respect to the murder of John Callahan, BS 1544-TE was registered at the Chateau Great Western motel in Provincetown, MA, with female companionship prior to source leaving. Source had advised writer that source would be in Provincetown for a few days. Registration was under source's true name and source is well known to the family which runs the motel. Source recalls dining at Pepe's Restaurant during his stay at Provincetown.

137 A- 4075.57

(1)- Boston
JC/sct
(1)

Exhibit 318—the document that "says it all"

     "John Martorano . . . Kevin Weeks, Pat Nee, James Martorano. He talked about how vicious and violent they were on the streets of Boston. And you have to sit there and ask yourself: Why are they still walking the streets? If they're so vicious and violent and our government knows about it, why are they out there right now?"

He was hardly a minute into his closing, and already he was repeating himself: "Why is it that the federal government, knowing how violent and brutal these men are, why is it they're still out there today?"

All through the trial, Brennan and Carney had concentrated their why-are-they-still-out-there rhetoric on Pat Nee. Now they were throwing in the other members of the gang, maybe to pad their arguments.

"What about Howie Winter? Was there ever a grand jury? Was there ever an indictment? Why?"

If the prosecution can "almost brag" about destroying the gang, he said, "then why did they let almost everybody go?"

Brennan had a couple of phrases that he would return to again and again. "Rogue agents"—that was almost everybody in the Boston FBI office. And "soldiers," as in soldiers of the Department of Justice. Not surprisingly, John Morris fit the bill. But so did Stevie Flemmi; that's why he was brought back from Montreal in 1974, because the FBI needed its "soldier" in the war against the Mafia.

Brennan paraphrased the testimony of former state police Col. Tom Foley to make the point about the FBI's corruption:

"The feds stymied our investigation of Whitey, got us investigated on bogus claims, tried to push me off the case, got me banished to a distant barracks, phonied up charges against other members of the State Police, lied to reporters, misled Congress, drew in the President of the United States to save themselves, nearly got me and my investigators killed."

Brennan tried to defend Fitzpatrick, as well as simultaneously appealing to any jurors paranoid about recent stories about governmental abuses at other agencies such as the IRS and the NSA.

"They'll crush you," Brennan said. "You saw what they did to Mr. Fitzpatrick. Twenty-two years, he leaves three years before his pension. They bully him, they berate him, they crush him. That's what happens if you're not with them, you're either with them or you're against them."

"Them." In the 1980's Whitey was most definitely a vital cog in what the late drug Charlestown drug dealer Joe Murray called "the machine." That was why Whitey could tell extortion victim Michael Solimando not to even think about going to any local cops in Boston, because he controlled them all.

But that was then, and this was now, and Whitey could do little more than suggest a rough script for his lawyers.

"The files don't show that he was an informant," Brennan said halfheartedly.

He became more animated when he got onto the subject of John Morris—"the same John Morris who drank so much he had the nickname 'Vino' in the underworld, and funny enough, he now works at a wine factory."

Actually, he had said he was a consultant, but close enough, for a closing.

"What does he say? He was compromised. Like he was Secret Squirrel, I was compromised. He was corrupt. He wasn't compromised, he was corrupt. He was as or more corrupt than John Connolly. He was with the whole lot of them. But he's with them, so he gets immunity. And you know what, he gets a pension that we're paying for because he's with them."

Them again. But this screed had another Bulger touch—the pension reference. All the Bulgers have always been obsessed with pensions. When Whitey was fired from his no-show job at the courthouse by John E. Powers, he complained bitterly to his gangster pals.

As Fat Harry Johnson explained it on a State Police wiretap, "Behind the job comes the pension."

And now John Morris had one—and his freedom. And Whitey had neither. It was as infuriating as Pat Nee's TV show.

Next Brennan blamed Morris for tipping Connolly to the fact that Halloran had become an FBI informant.

Carney leaves the courthouse with his mother after the closing

"He sent the word. He signed the death warrant when he sent that word, and he knew it."

Just as during the cross-examination of Morris, there was no mention of who actually executed the death warrant, not to mention Halloran and Donahue. Just as there was no mention of who "corrupted, not compromised" the pathetic Vino.

"Why is he getting immunity?" thundered Brennan. "Why is he getting a pension?"

In closing, Brennan echoed George Wallace's 1968 plea to "send them a message." Them.

"You can let them know, this isn't your government, this is my government. This is our government and there's going to be accountability, but there has to be accountability for each and every person, and this government is equally accountable. You tell them that."

Tell "them" that, whatever "that" means.

Next it was Carney's turn. Unlike Brennan, he would adopt a more folksy, personable persona, still denouncing the government and its witnesses, but adding at least a small human touch or two.

"Today I'm particularly nervous," the 61-year-old lawyer began, "because for the first time in my 35 years as a lawyer, my mother is in court watching me, and I'm going to try to not make that affect me too much."

Carney sounded like he'd gotten a few suggestions from another of the Bulgers—specifically, Billy. In his 1996 memoir, Billy had claimed that the evidence against his much-to-be-admired brother was "purchased."

Now Carney said, "The government is buying the testimony of these witnesses. Sounds pretty awful to put it that way, doesn't it? The government is buying their testimony. The witnesses are selling their testimony to the government."

He continued on, discussing immunity from prosecution and how it can be obtained, until finally Wyshak spoke up.

"I object to that, that's an incorrect statement of the law, your Honor."

"Overruled," the judge said.

"Unbelievable," Carney snapped, no longer Mr. Nice Guy. "Even getting speaking objections during my closing argument."

Carney asked the jury if they could believe John Martorano.

"What kind of moral character and values does he bring to the table? Well, let's consider what his job was. Professional killer. Probably don't see that too often on a résumé, but that's what John Martorano did. He was a professional killer . . . Lying to people is part of his job as a professional killer. John Martorano could only be such a good professional killer if he was such a good liar. Does a person with all this training give you pause? Can you trust him to tell you the truth?"

He reminded the jury that Martorano had described himself on *60 Minutes*, and in the courtroom, as a vigilante.

"I think you go a little earlier in the dictionary than 'vigilante,' I think you stop at 'psychopath' if you want to know who John Martorano is."

Carney said Whitey Bulger had no need to get involved in the World Jai Alai murders. He was making too much money in his hometown, Wards 6 and 7 of the city of Boston.

"James Bulger oversaw the criminal activities in South Boston, not in eastern Massachusetts, not in the entire city of Boston, not in Dorchester or Charlestown or Brighton or the South End, one neighborhood in Boston. And he made millions of dollars doing it. There, I've said it again! He didn't need to go beyond South Boston. It would be insanity for him to just decamp to Miami and try to take over World Jai Alai."

He returned to another theme from the opening—that Martorano had learned how to be an informant from Joe Barboza. He said Joe Barboza had framed four men for a murder "committed by Jimmy Martorano." He apparently meant Jimmy Flemmi, but he kept referring to "Jimmy Martorano." Wyshak might have objected, but he had already been chastised once by the judge.

But Carney was more concerned about Johnny than Jimmy Martorano.

"The prosecutors were willing to pay such a high price that Martorano could dictate to the government, I'm not going to testify against Howie Winter, I'm not going to testify against Patrick Nee, I'm not going to testify against my brother Jimmy. Unbelievable."

During his testimony, Martorano had said it "broke my heart" to learn that Whitey was a rat.

"I think if you did a CAT scan, you'd have trouble finding a heart in this guy. Do you think he really became a government witness because he had a broken heart? Yet he's willing to say that to you from the stand and tell you that was the truth."

Next he mentioned how Kevin Weeks threatened him from the witness stand when he asked Weeks what he'd do to anyone who called him a rat.

"Heck, first time ever in my career that a witness has said to me, 'Why don't you come outside and I'll show you what I'll do to you.' Yikes. Holy mackerel. I mean, they don't pay enough at court-appointed rates to be threatened by the witness to be taken outside."

But then he thanked Weeks for admitting that he lies about everything.

"May I kiss you, Mr. Weeks, for your candor?"

Then he began going over Weeks' testimony, beginning with the murder of Bucky Barrett.

"Jimmy Martorano came by with him. Why wasn't Jimmy Martorano called as a witness here by the government? Why didn't they give him a deal, like they gave everybody else? Why wasn't Patrick Nee ever called at this trial by the government? Why wasn't he offered a deal?"

Next, John McIntyre.

"Pat Nee received $20,000 the day before, and Pat Nee brought John McIntyre to his brother's house. Weeks threw McIntyre to the floor. Flemmi and Weeks buried the body. Isn't it interesting how many times you hear Patrick Nee or Patrick Nee's brother's house mentioned?"

Then he gave Weeks another needle—"I know he doesn't like it, but 'Two Weeks' is his nickname for a reason, because that's how quickly he made a deal."

But his mind wasn't really on Kevin Weeks.

"How bad did the prosecutors want the testimony of Kevin Nee?" He didn't even catch himself. A few seconds later, though, he said, "Kevin Nee—I mean Kevin Weeks wanted James Bulger never to be caught. And so he could include him in everything."

And then, once more: "Ask yourselves, would you trust Kevin Nee—I mean, Kevin Weeks?"

Carney couldn't hide his disdain for the prosecutors, especially Fred Wyshak. He joked about Stevie Flemmi's tendency to include Whitey in everything he did.

"What was the weather that day? It was raining, and Jim Bulger was my partner. What kind of car were you driving? Oh, I was driving a Ford

Bucky's widow Elaine Barrett leaves courthouse in tears

Fairlane, and Jim Bulger was my partner . . . All I can say is Mr. Wyshak paid a big price, but he got his money's worth in terms of how many times—"

Wyshak interrupted. "Your Honor, I object to this constant impugning of the prosecution. It's totally unprofessional."

"Overruled," the judge said. "Overruled."

Then he told the jury he wanted to "just take a look at two crimes in particular." The murders of Stevie Flemmi's two women, of course. Starting with his stepdaughter, Deb Hussey.

"He says, Oh, she just abused drugs, she was a drug addict, I tried to get her help. Do you think he helped her when she was a teenager where, as her stepfather, he had sex with her? Do you think that might be related to why Deborah Hussey spiraled down? What does he say? Oh, well, when I got back from the lam, she was a teenager and she was different. Well, no kidding. Little girls grow up to be teenagers. To Flemmi that became a green light. What does he say? Oh, she consented. Yeah, she consented. Do you think that was an appropriate consent? I mean, I can't even talk about it."

But then he did talk about it. He said Flemmi treated her like an abandoned puppy. He read once more from the testimony of her dying mother,

Stevie's common-law wife, Marion Hussey, in an earlier civil suit. He quoted Hussey saying that Stevie "slapped her around." He always told Marion, "She's no good, she's a slut, she's a whore, she's a prostitute, she's out there doing drugs."

He read how finally Deb had told her mother that she'd been—"Please read it," he asked the jury, "because I'm not going to say it."

After Stevie left the house in a rage, Hussey had testified, her daughter said to her: "'Ma,' she says, 'I'm not lying.' And I said, 'Debbie, I believe you.'"

Finally, he got to the discrepancies in Flemmi's recollections of how his partner had murdered Deb Hussey.

One time he said, "He put his hands around her throat and strangled her."

Marion Hussey

The next time Flemmi testified, "He took a rope and put it around her neck and strangled her with a rope."

The next time, "He got her in a headlock and killed her that way."

On the subject of Debbie Davis, he was more succinct—"I'm not going to go into the testimony in detail, because I'm sure you recall it." Or maybe Whitey just didn't want to hear it all again.

So Carney compared Stevie to a cockroach in the chowder and ended by quoting, of all people, Ralph DeMasi, wounded by a Winter Hill "broadside" from a hit car on Morrissey Boulevard that Whitey was driving.

Carney put DeMasi's quote up on the screen. He had been asked about the benefits of cooperating with the government.

"Yeah, guys are walking the street after they killed 20 people if they cooperated, and then you got other—one person who kills somebody and they put him in the electric chair. That's the way the government works. You kill 20 people, go testify against somebody, you can walk."

Then Carney closed, not with a statement of his client's innocence, but a plea to the jury.

"You have a power to stand up to governmental abuse."

WYSHAK WASTED no words in his rebuttal.

"Okay," he began. "So let's get back to reality here. The defense in this case wants you to take your eye off the ball. Although Mr. Carney can't bring himself at the end of his summation to say 'Find my client not guilty,' he suggests that you should essentially violate your oath as jurors here and issue some referendum on government misconduct . . . They're asking you to render some verdict that doesn't comply with the evidence but sends a message about how the big, bad government needs to learn a lesson from his case."

He pointed out that Flemmi and Bulger did not murder Deb Hussey until 1985—more than two years after she first told her mother Stevie had been raping her.

Then he added a detail that often went unnoticed, that after returning from Montreal in 1974, "there is not one murder where Mr. Flemmi has gone off on a detour and a frolic and killed somebody that wasn't part of the activity of this RICO organization. Once these men became partners, they did everything together."

Finally, Wyshak returned to a point he made very early in his own closing, that the reason these three men were testifying against Whitey was because they were his partners.

"Mr. Carney wants to call Mr. Martorano a psychopath, a pathological liar. Well, again, this is the defendant's criminal associate for 25 years. This is a man who Mr. Bulger murdered people with. This is a man with whom he associated; so too with Mr. Flemmi, so too with Mr. Weeks. As much as Mr. Carney wants to try to distance his client from these men, he cannot do it. They are together. They're part of the same criminal organization. They're partners. Everything they do they do together. That's the way this business worked."

Whitey's fate was now in the hands of the jury.

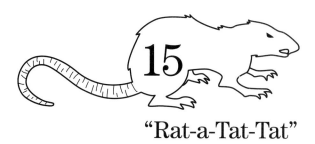

15

"Rat-a-Tat-Tat"

Whitey in the Air Force, early 1950's

The verdict was never in doubt. The only question was, how long would the jury of eight men and four women take to find him guilty, and on how many counts?

The jury took longer than most people thought they would. They got the case on Tuesday, Aug. 6, and returned a verdict on Monday, Aug. 12. In all, they deliberated 32½ hours before finding him guilty of 31 of the 32 counts against him.

In the most important racketeering count, Whitey was found guilty of the 11 of the 19 murders. The jury found "not proven" on seven of the earlier slayings, and came back with "no finding" on the one that mattered most to Whitey—the murder of Deb Davis.

He was, however, found guilty of murdering Stevie Flemmi's step-daughter, Deb Hussey. The survivors of the victims Whitey was not found guilty of slaying had mixed emotions after the verdicts were read.

Billy O'Brien, age 40, born a day or two after his father was machine-gunned on Morrissey Boulevard in 1973, denounced the "not proven" against his father.

"My father just got murdered 40 years later, again, today, in this courtroom."

The daughter of Buddy Leonard, murdered in 1975 when she was three years old, said the "not proven" finding made it almost seem as if her father had never existed. She was consoled by the daughter of Bucky Barrett, whom Whitey was found guilty of murdering in 1983.

Defense attorney J.W. Carney pronounced himself "very pleased" with the outcome, some 10 days after his client had denounced the trial as a "sham."

"Mr. Bulger knew as soon as he was arrested that he was going to die behind the walls of a prison or be injected with a chemical that would kill him," Carney said. "This trial was never about Jim Bulger being set free."

Jackie Bulger was chased into the parking lot across the street by a gang of reporters and cameramen, but never said a word. As usual, Billy Bulger was nowhere to be seen.

The prosecutors were naturally ecstatic that their long struggle was finally over. At the press conference outside the courthouse, U.S. Attorney Carmen Ortiz even answered a couple of questions for a Spanish-language reporter—in Spanish. She congratulated the "policia" for bringing Whitey to justice.

"I think justice prevailed," said prosecutor Fred Wyshak.

The *Boston Globe*, which almost single-handedly created the perniciously false image of Whitey as "the good bad guy," appeared schizophrenic in its coverage of the verdict.

In the main story the next day, the guilty verdict was described as having "laid to rest any romantic Hollywood notions about James Bulger as a Robin Hood figure."

The next Sunday, the lead editorial denounced the "mythology that glorified Bulger," without mentioning where that mythology had been most often promulgated. But now, the *Globe* continued, without any apparent appreciation of the irony, their one-time hero was widely recognized as "such a fraud . . . even in the most sympathetic precincts."

As for Whitey, he wouldn't have a chance to speak publicly until his sentencing in mid-November. But within a few weeks, a hand-written letter had appeared online, written to someone named Eric Morrison.

"The trial," Whitey wrote, "was a neck-tie party and a stacked deck from day one."

He seemed resigned to standing trial next in one of the death-penalty states, Florida or, more likely, Oklahoma.

"I expect the worst is yet to come," he said.

A couple of weeks later, he wrote another jailhouse missive about the raw deal he'd just received. "They demonized me to the nth degree," he scribbled from Plymouth.

He also complained about how he'd never been allowed to write to Catherine Greig—"a woman I was intensely in love with."

But in the September 11 letter, he saved most of his venom for "the Cook," Johnny Martorano.

"Twenty-three (sic) murders, 10 years in prison. Co-wrote bestseller, $70,000-$250,000 movie rights then another $250,000 when movie complete plus royalties. Free for years. No seizure of assets . . . I had no contact for years with the Confessed Killer who went into great detail about how he did it (the Wheeler and Callahan murders). 'But Whitey told me to do it' so he's been free for years."

Inside the courtroom on the day he was found guilty, he had tried to appear more positive. After the verdicts were read, Whitey glanced back toward his brother Jackie and gave him a thumbs-up. As the marshals led him out, Whitey smiled at Jackie and pointed at him.

But then a middle-aged woman in the gallery stood up. It was Cheryl Connors, daughter of Eddie Connors, slain by Whitey and Stevie in a phone booth on Morrissey Boulevard in 1975. A couple of weeks earlier, the prosecution had played a tape of a phone call Whitey made from Plymouth, in which he casually mentioned the machine-gun murder, twice using the phrase, "Rat-a-tat-tat."

Now Whitey, flanked by larger, younger deputy U.S. Marshals, was slowly making his way out of Courtroom 11. He couldn't see her, but Eddie Connors' daughter was yelling at her father's murderer.

"Rat-a-tat-tat, Whitey."

They were the last words Whitey would hear at his trial.

"Rat-a-tat-tat."

Whitey in the Ratmobile

Index